Study Guide

Church Resource for Classroom and Personal Study

OUR GREATEST OPPORTUNITY
What in the World is Missing?

SECTION I

Is Evangelism Going Out of Style? (Dec. 17, 2013)

According to Barna Research Group

- 9 out of 10 American Adults (86%), cannot accurately define the meaning of the "Great Commission"
- 7 out of 10 Adults have no clue what "John 3:16" means
- Barely one third of all adults (31%), know the meaning of the expression "the gospel"
- 52% of born-again Christians claimed they have shared their faith with a non-Christian this past year
- Busters (those between 18-33 years of age) are more likely than any other generation to share their faith with others; Barna's data shows that 48% of Busters shared their faith in the last year, compared to 58% of Boomers (those 34-52 years of age), 49% of Builders (those 53-71), and 53% of Seniors (those 72 years plus)
- Blacks (76%) are more likely than whites (52%) to report that they have shared their faith with someone in the past year

- 54% of Protestant, non-mainline attenders and 64% Baptist report that they have shared their faith with a non-Christian in the past year, compared to 42% of mainline attenders, and 33% of Catholics
- 7 out of 10 evangelicals acted on their faith last year (69%)
- Millennials rose from 56% in 2010 to 65% in 2013, ONLY 52% of Christians share their faith

POST- MODERN WORLD

Clues of Decline:

- ❖ **Preaching is not directed toward Evangelism**
- ❖ **The Church is well-intended to the community (social concerns, community goals)**

I. Matthew 28:18-20, "And Jesus came and spake unto them, saying, All power is given unto me in heaven and in earth. Go ye therefore, and teach all nations, baptizing them in the name of the Father, and of the Son, and of the Holy Ghost: Teaching them to observe all things whatsoever I have commanded you: and, lo, I am with you alway, even unto the end of the world. Amen"

Closer look

A. Vs. 18 – He spoke unto the disciples about his omnipotence that cannot be matched; "All power in heaven and earth." That covers it "All."

B. Vs. 19 – What are we to do? "Teach all nations." The Gospel message is the evangelistic message of the entire Bible; the death, the burial, and the resurrection.

C. Vs. 19 – "Baptizing them;" the identification of the Gospel message. The "New Life" (Rom. 6:3-4) ordained by the Godhead; the "Father," the "Son," and the "Holy Ghost."

D. Vs. 20 – "Teach them to observe all things whatsoever I have commanded you." John 14:26 tells us that we will be reminded by the Holy Ghost,

"...and bring all things to your remembrance, whatsoever I have said unto you." (the perpetual message with no mention of phasing it out)

E. Vs. 20 – The promise of His presence with Almighty power. The message and the commission has been sealed; "Thus Saith the Lord."

Our Greatest Opportunity

Salvation: How Important?

❖ **God's Eternal Plan**
❖ **God's Eternal Power**
❖ **God's Eternal Purpose**

II. Why is the Great Commission Our Greatest Opportunity?
   A. The Plan – Share His Eternal Promises:
   - I Peter 2:9, "But ye are a <u>chosen generation</u>, a royal priesthood, an holy nation, a peculiar people; that ye should shew forth the praises of him who hath called you out of darkness into his marvellous light."

   B. The Power – Prove His Personal Presence:
   - Romans 1:16, "For I am not ashamed of the gospel of Christ: for it is the <u>power of God unto salvation</u> to every one that believeth…"

   C. The Purpose – Share the Message, Make Disciples:
   - Matthew 4:19, "And he saith unto them, Follow me, and I will make you <u>fishers of men</u>."
   - Matthew 9:36-38, "But when he saw the multitudes, he was moved with compassion on them, because they fainted, and were scattered abroad, as sheep having no shepherd. Then saith he unto his disciples, The harvest truly is plenteous, but the labourers are few; Pray ye therefore the Lord of the harvest, that he will <u>send forth labourers into his harvest</u>."

**151,600 people die each day on this earth.
How many have accepted Christ?**

Wisdom from Jesus
Wisdom: Fruit from God

- ❖ **Book of Life**
- ❖ **Wisdom comes from Salvation**

III. Heaven is to be the destination.
    A. Accepting Christ will secure your place in Heaven because your name is written in the "Lamb's Book of Life":
- Revelation 20:15, "And whosoever was not found <u>written in the book of life</u> was cast into the lake of fire."
- Revelation 21:27, "And there shall in no wise enter into it (Heaven) any thing that defileth, neither whatsoever worketh abomination, or maketh a lie: but they which are written in the <u>Lamb's book of life</u>." – The unbeliever's name will not appear.

    B. There is an earthly wisdom from man, and a spiritual wisdom from God; Greek word "sofia" – insight, skill, intelligence.
- I Corinthians 2:4-5, "And my speech and my preaching was not with enticing words of man's wisdom, but in demonstration of the <u>Spirit and of power</u>: That your faith should not stand in the <u>wisdom</u> of men, but in the power of God." – Crafty ways are not God's ways, but wise ways are.
- Romans 8:16, "The Spirit itself beareth witness with our spirit, that we are the <u>children of God</u>." – We receive at salvation.

    C. Winning Souls started in the Old Testament; the enemy has always been cunning and subtle enough to trick mankind starting with Eve at the

"Tree of the Knowledge of Good and Evil." The "Tree of Life" is produced by the righteous as fruit to give to all that are captive by the enemy.
- II Corinthians 4:4, "In whom the <u>god of this world hath blinded the minds</u> of them which believe not, lest the light of the <u>glorious gospel of Christ</u>, who is the image of God, should shine unto them."
- Proverbs 11:30, "The <u>fruit of the righteous is a tree of life</u>; and he that <u>winneth souls is wise</u>."

D. Restoration to man is the main purpose on this cursed world, but only the wise are able to fulfill the commission.
- Psalms 126:6, "He that goeth forth and weepeth, <u>bearing precious seed</u>, shall doubtless come again with rejoicing, bringing his sheaves with him." – Wisdom has to be real as well as the burden to win the lost.
- Proverbs 2:10-11, "When <u>wisdom</u> entereth into thine <u>heart,</u> and knowledge is pleasant unto thy soul; <u>Discretion</u> shall <u>preserve</u> thee, understanding shall keep thee."
- John 4:34-38, "My meat is to do the will of him that sent me, and to finish his <u>work</u>. Say not ye, There are yet four months, and then cometh harvest? behold, I say unto <u>you</u>, <u>Lift up your eyes, and look</u> on the fields; for they are <u>white already to harvest</u>. And he that reapeth receiveth wages, and gathereth <u>fruit</u> unto life eternal: that both he that <u>soweth</u> and he that <u>reapeth</u> may rejoice together. And herein is that saying true, One soweth, and another reapeth. I sent you to reap that whereon ye bestowed no

<u>labour</u>: other men labored, and ye are entered into their <u>labours</u>."

List the name(s) of those you have witnessed to:
_____
_____

List the names of those you have led to Salvation:
_____
_____

TEST YOUR KNOWLEDGE
SECTION I

1. How many adults know the meaning of the Gospel?
   a. ¼ _____
   b. 1/3 _____
   c. ½ _____
2. How many born-again Christians claim they have shared their faith? _____ %
3. How many American adults can accurately define the "Great Commission?"
   a. 86% _____
   b. 60% _____
   c. 14% _____
4. Complete this verse found in Matthew 28:19 – "Go ye therefore, and _____ all nations, _____ them in the name of the _____, and of the _____, and of the _____ _____."
5. True or False: most preaching is directed towards Evangelism
   T___ F___
6. The "Great Commission" is God's Eternal P_____, Eternal P_____, and Eternal P_____.
7. According to research, how many people die each day? _____
8. Accepting Christ will get your name recorded in what book in Heaven?
   The _____ _____ of _____.
9. Soul-Winning started in the Old Testament. Write out two verses that support that truth:
   Prov. 11:30 --

   Psalms 126:6 –

10. Complete this verse found in John 4:35 – "Say not ye, There are yet four months, and then cometh _____? behold, I say unto you, _____ _____ _____, and _____ _____ the _____; for they are white already to harvest."

A Word to the Wise, From the Heart

SECTION II
Church – A Now-Day Phenomenon
- ❖ **Changes are Happening**
- ❖ **Salvation is Still Possible**

    I. The Church is exploding with new ways and ministries, but is salvation seen? Old churches will be left behind if not conformed to new worship styles
- II Timothy 3:5, "Having a form of <u>godliness</u>, but <u>denying the power</u> thereof: from such <u>turn away</u>."

  A. How can people turn away from a church, even if it is guilty?
- II Timothy 3:7, "Ever <u>learning,</u> and <u>never</u> able to come to the knowledge of the <u>truth</u>." – This passage talks of evil people, but churches are not evil, right? Satan can appeal to the flesh.

  B. The battle is real, but the lines have become blurred with programs, music, and sensational motives.
- Ephesians 6:12, "For we wrestle not against flesh and blood, but against <u>principalities</u>, against <u>powers</u>, against the <u>rulers</u> of the darkness of this world…"

  C. The commission has to be the mission of the Church to continue to keep the world out and the heart right.

- I John 2:15-16, "Love not the world, neither the things that are in the world. If any man love the world, the love of the Father is not in him. For all that is in the world, the lust of the flesh, and the lust of the eyes, and the pride of life, is not of the Father, but is of the world."

D. The barometer of Salvation should be moving up with the right church environment. The called out ones, "Ecclesia," honor the "House of the Lord."
- Romans 10:13, "For whosoever shall call upon the name of the Lord shall be saved."
- Hebrews 10:21-25, "And having an high priest over the <u>house of God</u>; Let us draw near with a <u>true heart</u> in <u>full assurance</u> of faith, having our <u>hearts</u> sprinkled from an <u>evil conscience</u>, and our bodies <u>washed</u> with pure water. Let us <u>hold fast</u> the profession of our faith without <u>wavering</u>; (for he is faithful that promised;) And let us consider one another to provoke unto love and unto <u>good works</u>: Not forsaking the assembling of ourselves together, as the <u>manner</u> of some is; but <u>exhorting</u> one another: and so much the <u>more,</u> as ye see the day approaching."

E. There are people honestly seeking a church today for the closest New Testament model because of the multiple types in our society. People need a lighthouse that is serious in the rescue of lost souls. A refuge from their old life, seeking anew.
- Matthew 5:14-16, "Ye are the <u>light</u> of the <u>world</u>. A <u>city</u> that is set on an hill <u>cannot</u> be hid. Neither do men light a candle, and

put it under a bushel, but on a candlestick; and it giveth <u>light unto all</u> that are in the <u>house</u>. Let your <u>light so shine</u> before men, that they may see your <u>good works</u>, and <u>glorify</u> your Father which is in heaven."

Consider the Heart

The Heart's Condition

❖ **The Heart is Complicated**
❖ **The Heart is the Center of Your Life**

II. Every human has a heart, saved or lost. The saved heart can still be imperfect even though regenerated by the Holy Spirit.
   A. The heart is complicated and can't always be trusted.
   - Jeremiah 17:9, "The heart is <u>deceitful</u> above all things, and <u>desperately wicked</u>: who can know it?"
     1. We are born with a sin nature – Rom. 5:19
     2. We have learned how to keep our feelings in – John 2:25
     3. We are guilty of sin; we have done the same as a lost person – Rom. 3:23
   B. Defusing your power to witness is the enemy's intention and hopefully you will not make any life changing decisions. (church members will be on the fence about soul-winning because of their heart's condition)
   C. Thoughts and imaginations come from the heart.
   - Foolishness – Ecclesiastes 8:11, "Because <u>sentence</u> against an evil work is not <u>executed speedily</u>, therefore the heart of the sons of men is fully set in them to do evil."
   - Madness – Ecclesiastes 9:3b, "…yea, also the heart of the sons of men is <u>full of</u> <u>evil</u>,

and <u>madness</u> is in their <u>heart</u> while they live…"
- Depravity – Jer. 17:9 (above)
- Extortion and Excess – Matthew 23:25b, "…For ye make clean the <u>outside</u> of the cup and of the platter, but <u>within</u> they are full of <u>extortion</u> and <u>excess</u>."
- Evil -- Mark 7:21-23, "For from <u>within,</u> out of the <u>heart</u> of men, proceed <u>evil thoughts</u>, adulteries, fornications, murders, Thefts, covetousness, wickedness, deceit, lasciviousness, an evil eye, blasphemy, pride, foolishness: All these <u>evil things</u> come from within, and <u>defile</u> the man."
- Unbelief – Hebrews 3:12, "Take heed, brethren, lest there be in any of you an <u>evil heart of unbelief</u>, in departing from the living God."

D. The heart is the center of your life. God can use our heart if we are wise and protect ourselves.
- Proverbs 2:10-11, "When <u>wisdom</u> entereth into thine <u>heart</u>, and <u>knowledge</u> is pleasant unto thy soul; Discretion shall <u>preserve</u> thee, <u>understanding</u> shall keep thee." The layers of your heart are only seen by God.
    1. The heart needs to be <u>guarded </u>to make the right decisions – Proverbs 4:23, "Keep thy heart with all <u>diligence</u>; for out of it are the <u>issues of life</u>."
    2. The heart <u>controls</u> what we say – Luke 6:45, "A good man out of the <u>good</u> <u>treasure </u>of his heart bringeth forth that which is <u>good</u>; and an evil

man out of the <u>evil treasure</u> of his heart bringeth forth that which is <u>evil</u>: for the <u>abundance</u> of his <u>heart</u> his <u>mouth speaketh</u>." My cup runneth over with words and I become a blessing or not.
   3. <u>Salvation</u> comes from the heart – Romans 10:10, "For with the <u>heart</u> man <u>believeth</u> unto righteousness; and with the mouth <u>confession</u> is made unto <u>salvation</u>."
E. God will <u>renew</u> your heart if you trust him and <u>yield</u> your heart unto him.
   1. Fix your heart upon the Lord – Psalm 112:7, "He shall not be afraid of evil tidings: his <u>heart</u> is <u>fixed</u>, <u>trusting</u> in the Lord."
   2. God's intention is to <u>build</u> your heart – Ezekiel 11:19-20, "And I will give them one heart, and I will put a <u>new spirit</u> within you; and I will take the <u>stony heart</u> out of their flesh, and will give them an heart of flesh: That they may <u>walk</u> in my <u>statutes,</u> and keep mine <u>ordinances</u>, and do them: and they shall be <u>my people</u>, and I will be their God."
   3. The heart has to be receptive – Luke 8:15, "But that on the <u>good ground</u> are they, which in an <u>honest</u> and <u>good heart</u>, having heard the word, <u>keep it,</u> and bring forth fruit with <u>patience</u>." Open your heart to His Word.
   4. The whole heart is required – Deuteronomy 6:5, "And thou shalt <u>love</u> the <u>Lord thy God</u> with all thine <u>heart</u>, and with all thy <u>soul</u>, and with all thy <u>might</u>."

Our biggest challenge is to not let our heart go astray by taking our focus off Almighty God. When God changes your heart, you can be instrumental in changing those around you.

I Corinthians 3:16-20, "Know ye not that ye are the temple of God, and that the <u>Spirit of God dwelleth</u> in you? If any man <u>defileth</u> the <u>temple</u> of God, him shall God destroy; for the temple of God is <u>holy</u>, which temple ye are. Let no man deceive himself. If any man among you seemeth to be wise in this world, let him become a <u>fool</u>, that he may be wise. For the <u>wisdom</u> of this <u>world</u> is <u>foolishness</u> with God. For it is written, he taketh the <u>wise</u> in their own <u>craftiness</u>. And again, the Lord knoweth the thoughts of the wise, that they are vain."

TEST YOUR KNOWLEDGE

SECTION II

1. Is it possible for churches today to change worship style, programs, etc. and lose focus on Salvation?
   Yes _____ No _____
2. The "Great Commission" has to be the _____ of the church.
3. The barometer of achievement in the church should be:
   a. Attendance _____
   b. Worship _____
   c. Salvation _____
4. Complete this verse found in II Timothy 3:5 – "Having a _____ of _____, but _____ the _____ thereof: from such turn away."
5. The Church should be a lighthouse for the lost who are seeking the truth.
   True ___ False ___
6. Thoughts and imaginations come from the heart- name at least three:
   _____, _____, _____.
7. Complete this verse found in Romans 10:10 – "For with the _____ man _____ unto righteousness; and with mouth _____ is made unto _____."
8. When God changes your heart, you can be instrumental in changing those around you.
   True _____ False _____

What are We Fighting For?

SECTION III
**There is Going to be a Fight –
Prepare for the Battle**
- ❖ **Put on the Whole Armor of God**
- ❖ **Ministry of the Holy Spirit**
- ❖ **Connect to God**

I. We are born physically weak and living in a cursed world.
   A. Put on the whole armor of God to be able to stand against the enemy.
   - Ephesians 6:12, "For we wrestle not against flesh and blood, but against principalities, against powers, against the rulers of the darkness of this world, against spiritual wickedness in high places." If God is on our side, then who can stand against us?

   B. The world system is in the middle of the flow; "cosmos," our world, is defined as: an ordered system of ideas, self-inclusive and harmonious.
   - Luke 21:34, "And take heed to yourselves, lest at any time your hearts be overcharged with surfeiting, and drunkenness, and cares of this life, and so that day come upon you unawares." It is easy to get caught up into things that seem harmless. Always be aware of the calling to fight.
   - II Timothy 2:4, "No man that warreth entangleth himself with the affairs of this

life; that he may please him who hath chosen him to be a soldier."
C. The Holy Spirit has a ministry to prepare the believer for battle and to overcome the flesh and the enemy.
- I John 4:3-4, "And every spirit that confesseth not that Jesus Christ is come in the flesh is not of God: and this is that spirit of antichrist, whereof ye have heard that it should come; and even now already is it in the world. Ye are of God, little children, and have overcome them: because greater is he that is in you, than he that is in the world." The Holy Spirit is prepared to:
  1. Possess the believer – Romans 6:4-7, "Therefore we are buried with him by baptism into death: that like as Christ was raised up from the dead by the glory of the Father, even so we also should walk in newness of life. For if we have been planted together in the likeness of his death, we shall be also in the likeness of his resurrection: Knowing this, that our old man is crucified with him, that the body of sin might be destroyed, that henceforth we should not serve sin. For he that is dead is freed from sin."
  2. Sanctify the believer – Romans 6:13-18, "Neither yield ye your members as instruments of unrighteousness unto sin: but yield yourselves unto God, as those that are alive from the dead, and your members as instruments of righteousness unto God. For sin shall

not have <u>dominion</u> over you: for ye are not under the law, but under grace. What then? shall we sin, because we are not under the <u>law</u>, but under <u>grace</u>? <u>God forbid</u>. Know ye not, that to whom ye yield yourselves <u>servants to obey</u>, his <u>servants</u> ye are to whom ye <u>obey</u>; whether of sin unto <u>death</u>, or of <u>obedience</u> unto <u>righteousness</u>? But God be thanked, that ye <u>were</u> the servants of sin, but ye have <u>obeyed from the heart</u> that form of doctrine which was delivered you. Being then made <u>free from sin</u>, ye <u>became</u> the servants of righteousness."

3. Edify Christ – Romans 6:8-12, "Now if we be <u>dead with Christ</u>, we believe that we shall also <u>live</u> with him: Knowing that Christ being raised from the dead dieth no more; <u>death</u> hath no more <u>dominion</u> over him. For in that he died, he died unto sin once: but in that he <u>liveth</u>, he <u>liveth unto God</u>. <u>Likewise reckon</u> ye also yourselves to be <u>dead indeed</u> unto sin, but <u>alive unto God</u> through Jesus Christ our Lord. Let not sin therefore reign in your <u>mortal body</u>, that ye should <u>obey</u> it in the <u>lusts</u> thereof."

D. The Holy Spirit is our cleansing agent, positioning agent, and glorifying agent to help us serve God.

- John 16:13-14, "Howbeit when he, the Spirit of truth, is come, he will <u>guide</u> you into all <u>truth</u>: for he shall not <u>speak</u> of himself; but <u>whatsoever</u> he shall <u>hear</u>, that shall he <u>speak</u>: and he will <u>shew you things to come</u>. He shall <u>glorify me</u>: for he shall <u>receive of mine</u>, and shall <u>shew it unto you</u>." We get direct orders from Heaven if we let the Holy Spirit guide.

E. "Apprehensive state of obedience to God," is defined as to follow, but not be sure, Spirit-led, but not be sold-out to God.
- Ephesians 4:23-24; "And be renewed in the spirit of your mind; And that ye put on the new man, which after God is created in righteousness and true holiness."

Connect to God

Seeking God Daily

- ❖ **Who is the Authority?**
- ❖ **Renew Your Life**

I. How does the flesh get the victory? Not totally convinced that we should let God lead?
- People have three separate parts which make up a whole person: we are a Trichotomy:
  - The Spirit – pneuma
  - The Soul – psuche
  - The Body – soma

  A. But when we are only using two parts, we are not following the Holy Spirit. These two dimensions are the soul and the body without the Spirit. We are not a dichotomy; a two part person.
  B. We will behave as a common lost person that has never been regenerated by the Holy Spirit (not saved) and can't follow God.
  C. The dimensions of the lost use: (he has a spirit but not regenerated)
     1. The soul – mind, body, and emotions.
     2. The body – sinful flesh.
     - I Corinthians 2:14, "But the <u>natural man</u> receiveth <u>not</u> the <u>things of the Spirit of God</u>: for they are <u>foolishness</u> unto him: neither can he <u>know them</u>, because they are <u>spiritually discerned</u>."

D. The saved person has the capability of serving God because he is spiritually connected to God. The trichotomy has three dimensions that should work together.
   - Titus 3:5-6, "Not by <u>works of righteousness</u> which we have done, but according to his mercy <u>he saved us</u>, by the <u>washing of regeneration,</u> and <u>renewing of the Holy Ghost</u>; Which he shed on us <u>abundantly</u> through <u>Jesus Christ our Saviour</u>."
E. In the Garden of Eden, Adam and Eve had a constant, direct connection to God until sin entered and they were consciously running from God.
   - Genesis 3:9, "And the Lord God <u>called unto Adam</u>, and said unto him, Where art thou?"
   - Genesis 3:10, "And he said, I <u>heard thy voice</u> in the garden, and I was <u>afraid</u>, because I was <u>naked</u>; and I <u>hid myself</u>."

   > **<u>The dis-connect began for all mankind.</u>**

F. God has not closed the channel of communication with man, all we have to do is choose to call upon Him.
   - Romans 10:13, "For <u>whosoever shall call</u> upon the name of the Lord shall be saved."
   - Philippians 4:6, "Be <u>careful</u> for <u>nothing</u>; but in <u>every thing</u> by <u>prayer</u> and <u>supplication</u> with thanksgiving let your <u>requests</u> be <u>made known</u> unto God."

G. The re-connect is a daily imperative to listen to God the Father. Think of this process as the
"Paradigm of Authority":

- **The Owner** – **The Spirit of God will instruct.**
    - **Your Spirit** – **Your choice to call on the Father showing that He is the Authority.**
    - **If you don't call on Him, Satan will intercept to be the Authority.**

- **The Manager** – **Will follow orders from the Owner.**
    - **Your Soul (mind, will, and emotions) – Who is the Spiritual Authority?**
    - **If Satan has intercepted, you will be in a two dimensional thinking pattern that leads to wrong decisions.**

- **The Employee** – **Will follow orders from the Manager.**
    - **Your Body** – **The Manager is making wrong decisions, the flesh (body) will now sin.**

H. Why do people sin? Because we have given over the Authority that belongs to God over to Satan. This will happen every day. The re-connect has to be made. God has given you a free will, and He will not force you, but you cannot live a Spiritual Christian life, making the right decision, and utilize the power of the Holy Spirit over sin, without Him being in the Authority position.

I. The correct terminology is "Soul Control." You are still saved, but you are allowing the enemy to instruct you, or call the shots. Be aware of this danger!

- Matthew 16:26, "For what is a man profited, if he shall gain the whole world, and lose his own soul? or what shall a man give in exchange for his soul?"

"Lose," in the Greek, "zemioo," means to injure, damage, or detriment.

1. Just because you are saved doesn't mean the devil can't lead you to sin. Soul Control is your mind, will, and emotions; your Soul, making wrong decisions.
2. By-passing the true Spiritual authority from God, you are giving up God's wisdom and instruction.
3. You don't have to lose control of your Soul.

- I Thessalonians 5:16-24, "Rejoice evermore. Pray without ceasing. In every thing give thanks: for this is the will of God in Christ Jesus concerning you. Quench not the Spirit. Despise not prophesyings. Prove all things; hold fast that which is good. Abstain from all appearance of evil. And the very God of peace sanctify you wholly; and I pray God your whole spirit and soul and body be preserved

<u>blameless</u> unto the coming of our Lord Jesus Christ."
J. The battle is on for the Soul, including yours, because you are vulnerable and live in a sinful world with a fallen agenda. What are we fighting for?
  1. Our own faithfulness to the Lord is at stake. The longer you are in the battle, the more you understand the "whole armour of God." (Eph.6) "...that ye may be able to <u>withstand</u> in the evil day, and having done all, to <u>stand</u>." Eph.6:13
  2. Transform your Soul by the Holy Spirit and the Word of God, being receptive to Him. This takes constant effort for a complete yielding. "And be not conformed to this world: but be ye transformed by the renewing of your mind...", Rom. 12:2
  3. Meditation and memorization will structure your mind and your life as God told Joshua that, "This book of the law shall not depart out of thy mouth; but thou shalt meditate therein day and night, that thou mayest observe to do according to all that is written therein: for then thou shalt make thy way prosperous, and then thou shalt have good success." (Josh.1:8)
     a. Use whole thoughts, such as "How to Conquer Lusts" – Romans 5-8
     b. "Temptations" – James 1
     c. "Grow Spiritually" – John 15
     d. "Develop Genuine Love" – I Corinthians 13
        ➢ God's thoughts are higher than ours. Strengthen your resolve and you will see a reshaping of your thoughts.

Pierce the Darkness

The World is in Darkness
- ❖ **Blindness**
- ❖ **Bring in the Light**

II. We wrestle against the "Rulers of the Darkness of this World" that are instructed to not let anyone cross the threshold of Salvation. It is a major struggle to pull a soul over to the light from a blinded state.
- A. Most people don't think that there are consequences and judgments in this life because they are hopelessly blind.
    - Isaiah 59:9-10, "Therefore is <u>judgment far from us</u>, neither doth <u>justice overtake</u> us: we wait for <u>light,</u> but behold <u>obscurity</u>; for brightness, but we <u>walk in darkness</u>. We <u>grope</u> for the <u>wall</u> like the <u>blind</u>, and we grope as if we had <u>no eyes</u>: we <u>stumble at noon-day</u> as in the <u>night</u>; we are in <u>desolate places</u> as <u>dead men</u>."
- B. God designed us with himself in mind with a spirit that needs regenerated by the Holy Spirit, and if not regenerated, we walk as dead with the spirit of man only to guide.
    - I Corinthians 2:11, "For what man <u>knoweth</u> the <u>things of a man</u>, save the <u>spirit</u> of <u>man</u> which is in him? even so the things of God knoweth no man, but the <u>Spirit of God</u>."
- C. This condition is not permanent because the devil is not our real God. He has done all to hide the truth.

- II Corinthians 4:3-4, "But if our <u>gospel be hid</u>, it is hid to them that are <u>lost</u>: In whom the <u>god of this world</u> hath <u>blinded the minds</u> of them which <u>believe not</u>, lest the <u>light of the glorious gospel of Christ</u>, who is the <u>image of God</u>, should <u>shine unto them</u>."

D. The only way to pierce the darkness is with the light of the gospel of truth. Paul and Barnabas were to be the light to the Gentiles. "For so the Lord hath commanded us, saying, I have <u>set thee</u> to be a <u>light</u> of the Gentiles, that thou shouldest be for <u>salvation</u> unto the <u>ends of the earth</u>." (Acts 13:47)
  1. Our commission is the same, to the <u>ends of the earth</u>.
  2. We are to <u>be the light</u>.

E. No matter to whom you witness, the spiritual boundaries are set. The threshold is the battleground. The middle-ground holds those ripe for harvest, discouraged by the enemy.

Worldly Wisdom ~~~~~~~~~~ Heavenly Vision

Human Promotions ~~~~~ Freedom from Bondage

Fleshly Ideas ~~~~~~~~~~~ Burdens Lifted

Sinful Pride ~~~~~~~~~~~~~~~ Sins Forgiven

Eternal Death ~~~~~~~~~~~~~~ Eternal Life

Lamb's Book of Life
- Revelation 3:20, "Behold, I stand at the door, and knock: if any man hear my voice, and open the door, I will come into

him, and will sup with him, and he with me."

TEST YOUR KNOWLEDGE
SECTION III

1. We are born and living in a cursed world, therefore we should put on the _____ _____ of _____.
2. Complete this verse found in Ephesians 6:11 – "Put on the _____ _____ ___ _____, that ye may be _____ to _____ against the _____ of the devil."
3. We are in a Spiritual Battle.
   True _____ False _____
4. Give the definition of the world system, "cosmos," that we live in:
   "_____
   _____
   _____."
5. Complete this verse found in II Timothy 2:4 - "No man that _____ _____ _____ with the affairs of this life; that he may please him who hath _____ him to be a _____."
6. The Holy Spirit has a ministry to do three things in the life of the believer. Name them:
   a. P_____
   b. S_____
   c. E_____ C_____
7. To follow God but, not be sure, to be Spirit led, but not be sold out, is termed: "A_____ S_____ of O_____ to G_____."
8. People are made up of three separate parts. Name them:
   a. _____ - pneuma
   b. _____ - psuche
   c. _____ - soma
9. The two dimensions of the lost person use the soul and body but not the Spirit of God.
   True_____ False_____

10. Who were the first individuals Spiritually connected to God? _____ and _____
11. The Spiritual channel of communication experienced a dis-connect when _____ entered into the world.
12. Complete this verse found in Genesis 3:10 – "And he said, I _____ thy _____ in the garden, and I was _____, because I was naked; and I hid myself."
13. The "Paradigm of Authority" is structured to help the Christian to follow God every day.
    ➢ The Owner is _____, as your Spiritual Authority.
    ➢ The Manager is your _____ , your mind will make decisions on whom you yield to. (God or Satan)
    ➢ The Employee is your _____, that takes orders from the Soul to now Sin or not.
14. Is it possible that the devil can have a daily "Soul Control" over a Christian? Yes____ No ____
15. Complete this verse found in Matthew 16:26 – "For what is a man _____, if he shall _____ the _____ _____, and lose his own _____? or what shall a man give in _____ for his soul?"
16. The Battle for the Soul includes the Christian, even though he/she is saved and has a desire to win Souls, one has to, according to Romans 12:2; R_____ your mind continually. Meditation on G_____ W_____ is required.
17. God designed the human with what part of him/her that needs regeneration?
    a. Spirit ___
    b. Soul ___
    c. Body ___
18. Complete this verse found in I Corinthians 2:11 – "For what man _____ the things of a man, save the

_____ of _____ which is in him? even so the things of _____ _____ no man, but the _____ of _____."

It's a Matter of Life or Death

SECTION IV
An Unspeakable Subject – Death and Eternity
- ❖ **Life or Death**
- ❖ **Heaven or Hell**
- ❖ **Reaching Out**
- ❖ **Seeds of Truth**

    I.   Where do you go when you die? The most asked question among children and adults.
- A. The answer is usually Heaven, because the thought of a place with no peace is unacceptable.
- B. A place where there is no more pain is acceptable.
- C. A place where the angels are is acceptable.
  - Job 14:14, "If a man <u>die</u>, shall he <u>live again</u>? all the days of my <u>appointed time</u> will I wait, till my <u>change</u> come."
  - Hebrews 9:27, "And as it is <u>appointed unto men once to die</u>, but after this the judgment."
- D. A time of death is not a popular subject.
  1. People feel challenged, mentally
  2. People feel vulnerable, emotionally
     - Job 14:10, "But man <u>dieth,</u> and <u>wasteth away</u>: yea, man <u>giveth up the ghost</u>, and <u>where</u> is he?"
- E. Times before the cross and the resurrection of Jesus Christ, all the dead went to a place named "sheol," in Hebrew, meaning grave.

Job did not understand life and death entirely, but he knew that there had to be more than just death.

Heaven or Hell

Where Will You Spend Eternity?
❖ Heaven and Hell are Real

    II.   Heaven and Hell are the reality for all people.

    A. Today we can understand the entire scope through God's Word that death is followed by judgment. The soul is eternal, whether saved and going to heaven or lost and going to hell, you will spend eternity somewhere.
- Ezekiel 18:4, "Behold, all <u>souls</u> are <u>mine</u>; as the soul of the <u>father</u>, so also the <u>soul</u> of the <u>son</u> is <u>mine</u>: the soul that sinneth, it shall die."

    B. The New Testament name for Hell is "<u>hades</u>," the place of the departed souls; and "ghennah;" the place of everlasting punishment. Jesus gave a brief description; "Where their worm dieth not, and the fire is not quenched." (Mark 9:44)

1. This is not the soul sleep, as some believe.
2. This is real existence forever.
- Luke 16:22-24, "And it came to pass, that the beggar died, and was <u>carried</u> by the <u>angels</u> into <u>Abraham's bosom</u>: the rich man also <u>died</u>, and was <u>buried</u>; And in <u>hell he lift up his eyes</u>, being in <u>torments</u>, and seeth Abraham afar off, and Lazarus in his bosom. And he cried and said, Father Abraham, have <u>mercy</u> on me,

and <u>send</u> Lazarus, that he may dip the tip of his <u>finger in water</u>, and <u>cool</u> my tongue; for I am tormented in this <u>flame</u>."
C. The place where Lazarus found safety with Abraham is named "paradeisos" in the Greek, meaning paradise; the destination of the saints.
1. The thief on the cross –
   ➢ Luke 23:43, "…To day shalt thou be <u>with me in paradise</u>."
2. Paul's third Heaven –
   ➢ II Corinthians 12:3-4, "And I knew such a man, (whether in the body, or out of the body, I cannot tell: God knoweth;) How that he was <u>caught up</u> into <u>paradise</u>, and heard unspeakable words, which is not lawful for a man to utter."
3. A message from Jesus to the churches–
   ➢ Revelation 2:7, "He that hath an ear, let him <u>hear</u> what the <u>Spirit saith</u> unto the <u>churches</u>; To <u>him</u> that <u>overcometh</u> will I give to eat of the <u>tree of life</u>, which is in the midst of the <u>paradise of God</u>."

Reaching Out

The Wall of Communication
❖ There Will be Resistance
❖ Reach for the Fruit

    III.   The wall of communication is present and is the biggest challenge to overcome.
        A. How do you reach people with the Gospel? <u>You graciously love them to the cross</u>.
        B. How much do you care about their lost condition?
- I Corinthians 9:22, "To the weak became I as <u>weak</u>, that I might <u>gain</u> the <u>weak</u>: I am <u>made</u> <u>all things to all men</u>, that I might by all means <u>save some</u>."

        C. People are defensively closed off to the truth. A barrier has been created because of so much undesirable and untrustworthy communication.
        D. To accept Christ as Savior has to be their own choice. You can't force anyone to the cross of Jesus Christ. The "ground" of the <u>heart</u> has to be cultivated first.
        E. There are seven steps a common person will experience; the soul-winner will observe these:
           1. Doesn't believe in God – Defiant
               a. Doesn't care about right and wrong
               b. Religion is a crutch
               c. To each their own
           2. Doesn't sin – As good as anyone else
               a. I am a good person

      b. I will give to charities
3. Loves life the way it is – The flesh comes first
      a. I will find all the pleasures
      b. The world's agenda is fine with me
4. Decided that churches are controlling – Strong-willed
      a. All they want is my money
      b. They also want my time
5. Heard of Jesus and Heaven – Starting to think
      a. Not in church, waste of time
      b. Believes in God
6. Been thinking about going to church – Open
      a. Not convinced it's relevant
      b. No real convictions
      c. Wants to go to Heaven
7. Ready to be Saved – Ripe
      a. Ripe to the point of listening
      b. The heart is open to the truth
      c. Need some answers

You can observe a person's spiritual condition by communication. Step up and meet the challenge of leading the person to the step of Salvation. This will be your fruit.

- Proverbs 11:30, "The <u>fruit of righteousness</u> is a tree of life; and he that <u>winneth souls</u> is <u>wise</u>."

F. The Hebrew word for "fruit" is "periy," (per-ee`), meaning reward, and the Greek word, in the New Testament is, "karpos," meaning, as plucked up.

- John 4:35-36, "Say not ye, There are yet four months, and then cometh harvest? behold, I say unto you, Lift up your eyes, and <u>look on the</u> <u>fields</u>; for they are <u>white already to harvest</u>. And he that <u>reapeth receiveth</u> wages, and gathereth <u>fruit</u> unto <u>life eternal</u>: that both he that <u>soweth</u> and he that <u>reapeth</u> may <u>rejoice together</u>."

Sowing the Seeds of Truth

Sowing is Required

- ❖ **The Field is the World**
- ❖ **The Wise Sower**
- ❖ **Genuine Salvation is Needed**

    IV.   Sowing is required, patience is needed.
       A. The Word of God has been sown in some places and there are places that never heard the Word and has not been sown.
- John 4:38, "I sent you to <u>reap</u> that whereon ye <u>bestowed no labour</u>: <u>other men</u> laboured, and ye are entered into <u>their</u> labours."

       B. The work has started and needs finished. Your forefathers started these great churches by sowing and reaping.
       C. Today we have technology that gives the soul-winner more opportunities to sow and reap:
          1. Online Bible trainings and messages
          2. Christian cinema
          3. Social media, phones, etc.
       D. Choose the ground carefully and effectively if you want a greater yield to your crop, as the farmer would say. The parable of the sower gives the never changing layout of the field.
- Matthew 13:3, "...Behold, a sower went forth to sow."
- Verses 4-23 give our layout of activity on the field:

Vs.4 "…some seeds fell by the way side, and the fowls came and devoured them up."

Vs.19 "When any one heareth the word of the kingdom, and understandeth it not, then cometh the wicked one, and catcheth away…"
No Follow-up

Vs.5 "Some fell upon stony places, where they had not much earth: and forthwith they sprung up, because they had no deepness of earth."

Vs.20 "…the same is he that heareth the word, and anon (soon) with joy receiveth it."

Vs.6 "And when the sun was up, they were scorched; and because they had no root, they withered away."

Vs.21 "Yet hath he not root in himself, but dureth for a while: for when tribulation or persecution ariseth because of the word, by and by he is offended."
Emotional Only not Saved

Vs.7 "And some fell among thorns; and the thorns sprung up, and choked them."
Vs.22 "…he that heareth the word; and the care of this world, and the deceitfulness of riches, choke the word, and he becometh unfruitful."
Priorities Not Right

Vs.8 "But other fell into good ground, and brought forth fruit, some an hundredfold, some sixtyfold, some thirtyfold."

Vs.23 "…he that heareth the word, and understandeth it; which also beareth fruit, and bringeth forth, some an hundredfold, some sixty, some thirty."

Yields Heart to God and His Word

    E. The wise sower will reap benefits from the field as well as personal growth. The sower's heart has to start on "good ground" to accept the word, nurture the word, and live out the word.

    F. When you handle the Word of God, it will pierce you as well; "…Sharper than any two-edged sword…" You will see more fruit in your life with an everlasting joy!

    G. The church will be affected by sowing and reaping positively or negatively; new life is required in every church because people die and move away.

    H. Nothing can replace genuine Salvation in a church; we can keep things lively with:
        1. Music
        2. Family Enrichment
        3. Stewardship
        4. Building Projects
        5. Youth Programs
        6. Senior Involvement
        7. Missions

    I. With no undercurrent of new life, the foundation will be compromised and weakened to a man-made movement.

    J. What will happen if the crop is not harvested on time?
        1. The fruit thereof will fall, die, and decay.
        2. People will go by the wayside not cultivated by the Word of God.

    K. The partnership with God and His word is vital for new life.
- John 15:5, "I am the <u>vine</u>, ye are the <u>branches</u>: He that <u>abideth in me</u>, and

I in him, the same <u>bringeth forth much fruit</u>: for <u>without me ye can do nothing</u>." **Our Life Source**

L. Jesus and the Father as another example:
- John 15:1, "I am the true vine, and my Father is the husbandman."

Draw life from Jesus and the Holy Spirit to supernaturally save the Hell-bound soul to eternal life. You can make a difference of life or death!

TEST YOUR KNOWLEDGE
SECTION IV

1. The most asked question among children and adults is: Where do _____ ____ when you _____?
2. Complete this verse found in Job 14:14 – "If a man _____, shall he _____ _____? all the days of my _____ _____ will I wait, till my change come."
3. All people have an _____ _____ but do not want to face the reality of death.
4. In the time before the cross and the resurrection of Jesus, all the dead went to a place called "_____," meaning the grave.
5. The New Testament term for Hell is "_____," and the place for everlasting punishment is "_____."
6. Complete this verse found in Luke 16:23 – "And in _____ he lift up his eyes, being in _____, and seeth Abraham afar off, and Lazarus in his bosom."
7. The place Lazarus found safety, in Abraham's bosom, now the destination we call Heaven, is called "_____?" (Luke 23:43, II Cor. 12:4, Rev. 2:7)
8. The wall of communication is the biggest challenge to overcome. The soul-winner will observe seven steps. Name these:
   a. Doesn't believe in _____.
   b. Doesn't _____.
   c. Loves life _____ _____ ____ ____.
   d. Decided that churches are _____.
   e. Heard of _____ _____ _____.
   f. Been thinking about _____ _____ _____.
   g. Ready to _____ _____.
9. Complete this verse found in Proverbs 11:30 – "The _____ of the _____ is a tree of life; and he that _____ _____ is _____."

10. The Word of God as seeds, has been _____ in places, and there are still _____ not _____.

11. Complete this verse found in John 4:36 – "And he that _____ receiveth wages, and gathereth _____ unto _____ _____: that both he that _____ and he that _____ may _____ together."

12. List some ways technology today has improved our opportunity to reach the lost: (name three) _____, _____, _____ etc.

13. A sower went forth to sow, according to Matthew 13:3; some seeds:

(match with corresponding verse)

Vs.4 _____   Vs.20 – fell in stony places
Vs.5 _____   Vs. 22 – fell among thorns

Vs.7 _____   Vs. 23 – fell into good ground

Vs.8 _____   Vs. 19 – fell by the wayside

14. What will happen if the crop is not harvested in time?
    a. _____ The fruit thereof will fall, die, and decay.
    b. _____ People will go by the wayside if not cultivated by the Word of God.
    c. _____ All of the above.

Does Anybody Know the Time?

SECTION V
Time - The Clock is Running Down
- ❖ **Elusive for Man**
- ❖ **Warning**
- ❖ **The Seasons of the Age**
- ❖ **In Times Like These**

I. Time is on everyone's mind.
   A. God invented time for His purpose and every allotted interval, "chronos," in the Greek, affects our world.
   B. There is no beginning or end for God, all things are eternal.
      1. Eternity Past – before God created the world.
      2. Eternity Present – the world from Genesis to Revelation.
      3. Eternity Future – God creates a new Heaven and earth.
   C. Time can be illusive for man to understand; but God can see all the aspects of eternity at the same time. (Omnipresent and Omniscient)
   D. The Bible tells us of "Eternal Life," but it is hard for man to comprehend anything past our earthly existence; but there will come an end to all things.
- Ephesians 1:10, "That in the <u>dispensation of the fullness of times</u> he might <u>gather</u> together in one <u>all</u>

things in <u>Christ</u>, both which are in <u>heaven</u>, and which are on <u>earth</u>; even in <u>him</u>."
- Revelation 21:1, "And I saw a <u>new heaven and a new earth</u>: for the <u>first</u> heaven and the <u>first</u> earth were <u>passed away</u>; and there was no more sea."

E. This earth, as we know it, is not in infancy, but in full maturity today. Like any other living organism there is:
1. Birth – Genesis, 4000 B.C.
2. Growth – Pre-Bethlehem, from 4000 B.C
3. Maturity – since Jesus came and ushered in Grace from the cross, (church age) over 2000 years.
4. Death – and rebirth in our case. (after judgment)

Warning

Sound the Alert
- ❖ **Churches Be Aware**
- ❖ **Christians Be Ready**

II.   The warning is present.
       A. We have been living in God's Grace, on life support for some time, but terminality exists.
- Matthew 24:36, "But of <u>that day</u> and <u>hour knoweth no man</u>, no, not the <u>angels</u> of heaven, but my <u>Father only</u>." God the father will determine the time for the final harvest. When the last soul accepts Christ, only He knows.

       B. In the days of Noah, people would not heed the preaching and warnings.
- Matthew 24:37-39; "But as the <u>days of Noe</u> were, so shall also the <u>coming</u> of the Son of man be. For as in the days that were <u>before the flood</u> they were eating and drinking, marrying and giving in marriage, until the day that <u>Noe entered into the ark</u>, And knew not until the <u>flood came</u>, and <u>took them</u> all away; so shall also the <u>coming of the Son of man be</u>."

Closer Look -

Vs.39; the word "knew," in the Greek, "ginosko," meaning, to be aware of, have knowledge, perceive, to be sure, to understand. They knew, but did not take Noah seriously.

C. People today are either not well informed or just not taking God's Word seriously, because the parallels of Noah's day and ours are similar.
- Genesis 6:5-6, "And God saw that the <u>wickedness of man</u> was great in the <u>earth</u>, and that <u>every imagination</u> of the <u>thoughts of his heart</u> was only evil <u>continually</u>. And it <u>repented</u> the Lord that he had made man on the earth, and it <u>grieved</u> him at his <u>heart</u>."

D. Unbelief is not an excuse to not accept reality. In Noah's day, they had not seen rain, but it came regardless.

E. Paul wrote to the Thessalonian church which had never seen a man fly.
- I Thessalonians 4:16-17, "For the <u>Lord</u> himself shall <u>descend from heaven</u> with a shout, with the voice of the archangel, and with the trump of God: and the dead in Christ shall <u>rise first</u>: Then we which are <u>alive</u> and <u>remain</u> shall be <u>caught up together</u> with them in the <u>clouds</u>, to <u>meet</u> the <u>Lord in the air</u>: and so shall we <u>ever</u> be with the Lord."

This truth can't be too difficult to believe of our capabilities in this present age. People are aware of:
1. Space themes on the big screen.
2. Supernatural themes with twists of reality.
3. Prophetic themes in the airways.

The Seasons of the Age

Times Past - Times Are Here

III. The Season of the Age is upon us.
    A. Time has become routine with no urgency to act on anything. With no thought of Chronology at all.
        1. Time to get up
        2. Time to go to work or school
        3. Time to eat
        4. Time to play
        5. Time for bed
    B. Time for the Church to awake and notice.
- Ephesians 5:14-17, "Wherefore he saith, <u>Awake</u> thou that <u>sleepest</u>, and <u>arise from the dead</u>, and <u>Christ</u> shall give thee <u>light</u>. See then that ye walk <u>circumspectly</u>, not as <u>fools</u>, but as <u>wise</u>, <u>Redeeming the time</u>, because the <u>days are evil</u>. Wherefore be ye not <u>unwise</u>, but <u>understanding</u> what the <u>will</u> of the <u>Lord</u> is." Many would agree that the days are evil with shootings, bombings, and evil troops trying to terrorize the entire world.

    C. Take advantage of the pre-tribulation age, not just accepting the times as people are dying and lost for eternity, but be proactive. The Holy Spirit is not finished rescuing souls from the enemy, recovering lives from error into awakening into the truth.

The Time is Now.
- Ecclesiastes 3:1, "To every thing there is a season, and a time to every purpose under the heaven."
- Ecclesiastes 3:7-8;"A time to rend, and a time to sew; a time to keep silence, and a time to speak; A time to love and a time to hate; a time of war, and a time of peace." These times and seasons are purposed from God. We can't choose to be in another time as well as we can't choose to be born.

The Coming of Christ is inevitable as the Church Age is waxing old. Revival of the flames of yesteryear need fanned because the Church has become a glowing ember.

Services Past:

1. Had people walking the aisles at invitation getting Saved.
2. Preachers proclaimed the unapologetic Gospel of Truth and Sin.
3. Heaven and Hell were the topics that touched Souls with a time of decision.
4. Men prayed before the services for people to accept Christ.
5. Families had a Godly dad that would bring their children to church and a Godly mother to raise them.
6. The anthems of Victory in Jesus rang through the airways.
7. We couldn't wait for Sunday night.
    "I am come to send fire on the earth; and what will I, if it be already kindled? But I have

a <u>baptism</u> to be <u>baptized with</u>; and how am I <u>straitened</u> till it be <u>accomplished</u>! Suppose ye that I am come to give <u>peace on earth</u>? I tell you, <u>Nay</u>; but rather <u>division</u>." (Luke 12:49-51)

Evangelism is that Fire.

In Times Like These

Weapons Ready
- ❖ **The Spiritual Battle**
- ❖ **Jesus is Our Greatest Weapon**

IV. In Times of the Present
  A. How can people fare the spiritual burdens of today's challenges and hardships?
  - Nehemiah 4:17, "<u>They which builded</u> on the wall, and they that <u>bare burdens</u>, with those that <u>laded</u>, <u>every one</u> with <u>one of his hands wrought in the work</u>, and with the <u>other</u> <u>hand held a weapon</u>." Unlike this crew, we are not building a wall, but plowing a field. The devil thinks he owns the territory we are working on.

  B. Expect Resistance from the enemy as a Church effort.
  1. Be realistic about the times we are living in.
  2. Be aware that the enemy will try to divide the group.
  3. Be prayerful for the power to witness.
  4. Regain the power of the Lord Jesus Christ to resist the devil.

  C. Satan knows his time is short and he will be extreme.
  - I John 2:18, "Little children, it is the <u>last time</u>: and as ye have heard that <u>antichrist</u> shall come, even now are there <u>many antichrists</u>; whereby we <u>know that it is the last time</u>."

D. Our Greatest Weapon is the Lord Jesus Christ.
- John 14:6, "Jesus saith unto him, I am the <u>way</u>, the <u>truth</u>, and the <u>life</u>: no man <u>cometh</u> unto the Father, but by me."
1. The "Way" – not another worldly, lustful, fleshly way or program.
2. The "Truth" – the devil swayed Eve with a lie; the truth is not a thing, but a person.
3. The "Life" – decisions made for God's will and agenda. "If you give the devil an inch, he will become a ruler." What decisions can you make for God if the enemy controls your soul? Not losing your Salvation, but "Soul Control." (Section 3) You are listening to the wrong authority to misdirection; partly of your flesh, mostly of the enemy.

E. Open Season on churches and Christians who compromise, practice self-absorption, and lose the purpose for the Church.
- I Peter 5:7-11, "<u>Casting</u> all your <u>care upon him</u>; for he <u>careth for you</u>. Be <u>sober</u>, be <u>vigilant</u>; because your <u>adversary the devil</u>, as a <u>roaring lion</u>, walketh about, <u>seeking whom he may devour</u>: Whom <u>resist steadfast in the faith,</u> <u>knowing</u> that the same <u>afflictions</u> are <u>accomplished in your brethren</u> that are in the <u>world</u>. But the <u>God of all grace</u>, who hath called us unto his eternal glory by Christ Jesus, after that ye have suffered a while, make you <u>perfect, stablish, strengthen, settle you</u>.

To him be glory and dominion for ever and ever. Amen."
F. The enemy has helpers in every area of society influencing our culture. The Church is no exception when certain people have crept in unaware to do the enemy's bidding in the face of righteousness.
G. The example of Jesus was to lay down His life for others, as He sacrificed His life on the cross for us. The time calls for getting our minds on others to secure their Salvation.
- Romans 13:10-12, "Love worketh no ill to his neighbor: therefore love is the fulfilling of the law. And that, knowing the time, that now it is high time, to awake out of sleep: for now is our salvation nearer than when we believed. The night is far spent, the day is at hand: let us therefore cast off the works of darkness, and let us put on the armour of light."

TEST YOUR KNOWLEDGE
SECTION V

1. There is no beginning for God, all things are eternal:
   a. Eternity P_____
   b. Eternity P_____
   c. Eternity F_____
2. There will come an end to all things as we know it today. True _____ False _____
3. Compete this verse found in Revelation 21:1 – "And I saw a _____ _____ and a _____ _____: for the _____ heaven and the _____ earth were _____ _____; and there was no more sea."
4. Our earth today is in full maturity, like any other living organism. There are three cycles before death:
   a. B_____ - (Genesis, 4000 B.C.)
   b. G_____ - (Pre-Bethlehem, from 4000 B.C.)
   c. M_____ - (Church Age, over 2000 years since the cross)
5. God will determine the time for the final harvest, when the last Soul will be saved. Man knows when that time is. True _____ False _____
6. Complete this verse found in Matthew 24:36 – "But of _____ _____ and hour _____ _____ _____, no, not the angels of heaven, but my _____ _____."
7. Jesus compared the last days as the days before the _____ when _____ preached the warning of God.
8. People are heeding God's Word today and taking Him seriously of the end times. True _____ False _____
9. Complete this verse found in Genesis 6:5 -- "And God _____ that the _____ of _____ was great in the earth, and that every _____ of the thoughts of his _____ was only _____ _____."

10. Time of the Church Age will end at Rapture. True _____ False _____
11. Name the series of events the world <u>will</u> go through according to Bible prophecy:
    a. R_____
    b. T_____
    c. M_____
12. Complete this verse found in Ephesians 5:16 – "Redeeming the _____, because the days are _____."
13. According to Luke 12:49, Jesus said he came to send "_____ on the earth?"
14. Antichrists are upon the earth now. True _____ False _____
15. Complete this verse found in I John 2:18 – "Little children, it is the _____ _____: and as ye have heard that _____ shall come, even now there are many _____; whereby we know that it is the _____ _____."

Here Comes the Judge

SECTION VI
All Have Sinned
- ❖ **Be Prepared**
- ❖ **All are Tested**
- ❖ **Eternity is Real**
- ❖ **Judgment Awaits**

I. There Will be a Test.
   A. Nobody likes to be tested, but tests are required in life. Schools, jobs, law, and the Lord will test you, so be ready.
   B. Some confuse being tested with being judged because they do not want to accept consequences for their actions.
   C. When the word Sin is mentioned, it will trigger a defensive mental state of avoiding the subject altogether.
   D. There are two meanings for Sin in the Old Testament:
      1. chata – to miss the mark, to sin against God
      2. chattath – an offense with penalty
   E. The New Testament has similar words for Sin:
      1. harmartia – to miss the mark
      2. harmartano – an offense with penalty
   F. The idea leads us to realize that you can try to improve or intentionally ignore any boundaries and sin against God with malice.

- James 4:17, "Therefore to him that <u>knoweth to do good,</u> and <u>doeth it not,</u> to him it is <u>sin</u>."
G. Thank God for the Grace according to Romans 5:20, "...But where sin abounded, grace did much more abound." We are going to sin with our ever-shifting soul.
H. Merits do not cancel out sin, you will still reap what you sow. Shall we continue in sin, that grace may abound? **God forbid.**
I. If the Christian has an opportunity to witness to a lost person and avoids the Holy Spirit's urging, is it sin?
    1. God knows if you are willing to serve Him in this capacity.
    2. He knows who needs to be saved and how long they have to live.
J. Jesus came to this earth to die for all of mankind.
    - Luke 19:10, "For the Son of man is come to <u>seek</u> and to <u>save</u> that which was <u>lost</u>."
    - II Corinthians 5:20, "Now then we are <u>ambassadors for Christ,</u> as though <u>God did beseech you</u> by us: we pray you in <u>Christ's stead,</u> be ye reconciled to God." We are trying to bring people to God in Salvation.
K. Our message and mission rests upon the meaning of two verse:
    - ➢ **"For the wages of sin is death; but the gift of God is eternal life through Jesus Christ our Lord." Romans 6:23**

➢ **"And as it is appointed unto men once to die, but after this the judgment." Hebrews 9:27**
Write out the difference between eternal death and eternal life:

_____

_____

Remember the Soul is eternal and there is a judgment.

Eternity is Real

Eternity Future is Facing All
❖ **Heaven**
❖ **Hell**

II.   Eternity is Real.
      A. Everyone wants to go to Heaven, and Hell is a place of those with good intentions.
      B. Get Right or get Left; get right with God now, or get left behind by death or Rapture.
      C. You can't decide your future after you die. If you could, it would be very clear what it would be.
- Luke 16:23, "And in <u>hell he lift up his eyes</u>, being in <u>torments</u>, and <u>seeth</u> Abraham afar off, and Lazarus in his bosom." The rich man was very aware of his torment and situation. No party with friends or comfort at all.

      D. Some would say that Hell is on earth, but they could not be more incorrect:
         1. Christians exist here, there are none in Hell.
         2. I can quench my thirst here, not in Hell.
         3. The Gospel is preached here, not in Hell.
A Christ-less Hell is the most valid expression because Jesus is considered to be the bridge; the only way, the truth, and the life, and nobody comes to the Father but by Jesus.
      E. God is everywhere, which makes Him omnipresent.

- Psalm 139:8, "If I ascend up into heaven, thou art there: if I make my bed in hell, behold, thou art there." This doesn't mean that everyone is where He is, it is not a passage into Heaven. The day of judgment will determine our location of eternal existence. Our earthly decisions will determine our position with God.

F. God does not want to condemn the world, so through His Son, He gives opportunity to be saved.

- John 3:16-18, Hebrews 9:27
    1. God does not want to see eternal death for any of His creation. He loves the world and sent His Son.
    2. His gift is free of charge and eternal for us.
    3. Judgment is sure after death, not altered in any way.

Judgment Awaits

Judgment is Real
- ❖ **Trial of Works**
- ❖ **Rewards**
- ❖ **Book of Life**

   III.   There are Two Judgments.
       A. The Judgment Seat of Christ; "…for we shall all stand before the judgment seat of Christ." Romans 14:10 (spoken to Christians trying to judge their brother)
- I Corinthians 3:11-15, "For other <u>foundation can no man lay</u> than that is laid, which is Jesus Christ. Now if any man <u>build upon</u> this <u>foundation</u> gold, silver, precious stones, wood, hay, stubble; Every man's <u>work shall be made manifest</u>: for <u>the day shall declare it</u>, because it shall be <u>revealed by fire</u>; and the <u>fire</u> shall <u>try every man's work</u> of what <u>sort</u> it is. If any man's <u>work abide</u> which he hath built thereupon, he shall <u>receive a reward</u>. If any man's <u>work shall be burned</u>, he shall <u>suffer loss</u>: but he himself shall be <u>saved;</u> yet so as by fire."
  1. Referred also as the "Reward Seat" or "Bema Seat," "Heaven is my throne, and earth is my footstool." Acts 7:49. This throne Judgment is for rewards in Heaven, those written in the "Lamb's Book of Life."
  2. The unsaved are excluded in Revelation 21:27, "And there shall in

no wise enter into any thing that defileth, neither whatsoever worketh abomination, or maketh a lie: but they which are written in the Lamb's book of life."
3. A threshold passage which distinguishes saved from lost found in Galatians 5, which lists the works of the flesh, (unsaved) and the Spiritual Fruit of the Saved.
- Galatians 5:19-24, "Now the works of the flesh are manifest, which are these; Adultery, fornication, uncleanness, lasciviousness, Idolatry, witchcraft, hatred, variance, emulations, wrath, strife, seditions, heresies, Envyings, murders, drunkenness, revellings, and such like: of the which I tell you before, as I have also told you in time past, that they which do such things shall not inherit the kingdom of God. But the fruit of the Spirit is love, joy, peace, longsuffering, gentleness, goodness, faith, Meekness, temperance, against such there is no law. And they that are Christ's have crucified the flesh with the affections and lusts."
- These are the ones who belong to Christ who will be caught up in rapture; "For if we believe that Jesus died and rose again, even so them also which sleep in Jesus will God bring with him." (I Thessalonians 4:14)

The first death, followed by Eternal Life.

B. The Great White Throne judgment;

- Revelation 20:11-15, "And I saw a <u>great white throne</u>, and him that sat on it, from whose face the earth and the heaven fled away; and there was found no place for them. And I saw the dead, small and great, stand before God; and the <u>books were opened</u>: and another book was opened, which is the <u>book of life</u>: and the <u>dead were judged</u> out of those things which were written in the books, according to their <u>works</u>. And the sea gave up the dead which were in it; and death and hell delivered up the dead which were in them: and they were <u>judged</u> every man according to their <u>works</u>. And <u>death and hell</u> were <u>cast</u> into the <u>lake of fire</u>. This is the <u>second death</u>. And whosoever was not found written in the book of life was cast into the <u>lake of fire</u>."
    1. The Bible is crystal clear here, that these judged are not saved and they are categorized with the eternal dead.
    2. The lake of fire now is their eternal destination.

    This is the second death; they died once on earth to be brought here to pronounce death forever.
C. Jesus will be the judge at both judgments;
    - Revelation 21:5-6, "And he that <u>sat upon the throne</u> said, Behold, I make all things new. And he said unto me, Write: for these words are true and faithful. And he said unto me, It is done. I am <u>Alpha and Omega</u>, the <u>beginning</u> and the <u>end</u>. I will give unto him that is athirst of the fountain of the water of life freely."

Eternity in Heaven is sure, and living with our Savior throughout eternity is the best reward anyone could receive. Our job is to share the good news of this place.

"And the Spirit and the bride say, Come. And let him that heareth say, Come. And let him that is athirst come. And whosoever will, let him take the water of life freely." Revelation 22:17

TEST YOUR KNOWLEDGE
SECTION VI

1. There are two terms for sin in the Old Testament as well as the New Testament.
    a. chata (OT), harmartia (NT) are defined: to_____
    b. chattah (OT), hamartano (NT) are defined: an_____
2. Complete this verse found in James 4:17 – Therefore to him that _____ to do _____, and _____ it _____, to him it is _____."
3. Complete this verse found in Romans 5:20b – "...But where _____ _____, _____ did much _____ abound."
4. "Shall we continue in sin that grace may abound? _____ _____" (Rom. 6:2a)
5. If the Christian has an opportunity to witness to the lost person, and he/she avoids it, is this sin? Yes _____ No _____
6. What is the true meaning of Eternal Death and Eternal Life? (check one)
    a. The soul is eternal and will go to Heaven or Hell _____
    b. Jesus died for everyone, so all have eternal life. _____
    c. Eternal death means that you just don't exist, and the few of the earth are chosen for eternal life in Heaven. _____
7. The message and the mission rest upon the meaning of two verses. Name these verses:
    a. _____ b. _____
8. Some would say that Hell is on earth, but why is this incorrect?

a. Christians_____
   b. I can _____
   c. The Gospel_____
9. There are two judgments found in the Bible; what are these?
   a. _____(Rom.14:10)
   b. _____(Rev.20:11)
10. Who will be judged at these thrones?
    a. S_____ - what judgment?
    _____
    b. L_____ - what judgment?
    _____
11. Complete this verse found in Revelation 20:15 – "And _____ was _____ _____ written in the _____ of _____ was cast into the lake of fire."
12. Who is sitting upon both thrones according to Revelation 21:5-6? _____ _____
    "I am the _____ and _____, the beginning and the end."

Take Up Thy Cross

SECTION VII
Marching Orders
- ❖ **Courage**
- ❖ **Fear Not**
- ❖ **Lift Up Thy Cross**

I.   Be of Good Courage.
    A. The Great Commission of the New Testament has a parallel from the Old Testament; the book of Joshua captures God's direct commission after the death of Moses.
- Joshua 1:2-3, "Moses my servant is dead; now <u>therefore arise go over</u> this Jordan, thou, and all this people, unto the <u>land</u> which I do <u>give</u> to them, even to the children of Israel. Every place that the sole of your foot shall tread upon, that have I given unto you, as I said unto Moses."
- Joshua 1:9, "Have not I <u>commanded thee</u>? <u>Be strong and of a good courage</u>; be <u>not afraid</u>, neither be thou dismayed: for the Lord thy God is <u>with thee</u> whithersoever thou goest."
  1. Direct from God.
  2. Promise from God.
  3. Presence of God.

    B. Be sure that God wants us to march upon this earth with His Word, spreading the

Gospel, sharing Hope for mankind to every living Soul.
C. "Courage" here is the Hebrew word, "amats," which means to be alert, steadfast minded, and strong. We could use the thoughts of bravery, as recorded in I Peter 5:8, "<u>Be sober</u>, <u>be vigilant</u>; because your adversary the devil, as a roaring lion, walketh about, seeking whom he may devour."
D. There are no rules or limitations, he will try to destroy you physically and spiritually.
>"The thief cometh not, but to steal, and to kill, and to destroy..." (John 10:10)
>He will catch you unaware – not paying attention.

   1. He will go for your weaknesses and tempt you.
   2. Make you doubt and question God's Word.
   The enemy's whole purpose is to keep you from your purpose by redirecting your strategy, distracting you into serving the flesh; total compromise.

"A <u>double minded</u> man is <u>unstable in all his ways</u>." James 1:8

E. Power, fame, and fortune are the makeup of his worldly engine to drive you away from God in a mighty fashion.
   - I John 2:15-16, "<u>Love not the world</u>, neither the <u>things that are in the world</u>. If any man love the world, the love of the <u>Father</u> is not in him. For <u>all</u> that is in the world, the <u>lust of the flesh</u>, and

> the <u>lust of the eyes</u>, and the <u>pride of life</u>, is not of the <u>Father</u>, but is of the <u>world</u>."

F. Plan your work and work your plan, most of all, renew constantly your mental will to move forward.

- Romans 12:2, "And be not <u>conformed</u> to this <u>world</u>: but be ye <u>transformed</u> by the <u>renewing of your mind</u>, that ye may <u>prove</u> what is that <u>good</u>, and <u>acceptable</u>, and <u>perfect, will of God</u>."

Be prepared to take on the wiles of the devil.

Fear Not

Fear is Deceptive

II. Be Not Afraid
   A. Fear is only inflated by the enemy to keep us from God's agenda.

   False **E**vidence **A**ppearing **R**eal
   1. Jesus said to Peter in Matthew 14:29, "Come."
   2. Peter saw the effects of the wind, he began to sink, "...O thou of little faith, wherefore didst thou doubt?" Matthew 14:31
   "But straightway Jesus spake unto them, saying, Be of good cheer; it is I; be not afraid." Mat. 14:27
   3. Even when the Lord assures the Christian that it will be alright, we will doubt and fear.
   B. There are only two natural fears for a human:
   1. The fear of loud noises – you can be absolutely relaxed, and a sudden loud noise will shake every nerve in your body.
   2. The fear of falling – you can be sleeping, having a wonderful dream and find yourself falling from some steep entity, and wake up with a jolt of terror.
   C. Natural fears are not Spiritual fears;
   1. The mind plays on the psyche as if you had your ego suddenly stolen; not in control of surroundings.

2. Our self-pride is shattered and caught off guard leaving you defenseless; not in control of surroundings.
3. Mankind has fear of not being in control, therefore he shies away from spiritual situations.
4. We can accept our natural fears, but not our spiritual fears.

    "And when the disciples <u>saw him</u> walking on the sea, they were <u>troubled,</u> saying, It is a <u>spirit</u>; and they <u>cried out for fear</u>." Mat. 14:26.

    Does this mean we are afraid of the devil or demons?

D. Fear only God because the devil has no real power over you, he just knows that you are human.

- Matthew 10:28, "And <u>fear not them</u> which <u>kill the body</u>, but are not able to <u>kill</u> <u>the soul</u>: but rather <u>fear him</u> which is able to <u>destroy both soul</u> <u>and body</u> <u>in hell</u>."

E. We can't go it alone. We need the Holy Spirit to guide, discern, and fill our hearts with clear instruction.

- John 16:13-14, "Howbeit when he, the <u>Spirit of truth</u>, <u>is come</u>, he will <u>guide</u> you into <u>all truth</u>: for he shall not speak of himself; but whatsoever he shall hear, that shall he speak: and he will <u>shew you things to come</u>. He shall <u>glorify me</u>: for he shall <u>receive of mine</u>, and shall shew it unto you." You and the Holy Spirit will glorify Christ together with instruction, inspiration, and heavenly truth.

Lift Up Thy Cross

Your Personal Cross
- ❖ **The Message**
- ❖ **The Stand**
- ❖ **The Success**

III. Lift up Your Cross.
A. To lift up the cross, you have to exchange your life to bear it properly.
- Matthew 16:24-25, "Then said Jesus unto his disciples, If any man will <u>come after me</u>, let him <u>deny himself</u>, and <u>take up his cross</u>, and follow me. For whosoever will <u>save his life shall lose it</u>: and whosoever will lose his life for my sake shall <u>find it</u>."
  1. Jesus did not refer to the cross as His own, but as your own.
  2. The more your cross is lifted, the more people will see Jesus and less of you.
  3. A new identity will appear to one that now holds the cross.

B. The message of the cross is the most powerful message ever heard. NO other message has:
  1. Eternal rewards
  2. A sacrificial foundation
  3. A soul-changing purpose
  4. A love motivated power
  5. A timeless endurance

Jesus came, died on the cross, rose again, and offers eternal life to all that believe.

C. Why would the enemy be offended with this message? What does the Bible tell us?
   1. Satan claimed victory in the Garden of Eden with Adam and Eve; sin entered into the entire world.
   2. He could now introduce sinful and devilish standards to all mortals.
   3. He has blinded the minds of people who will defend his worldly agenda to the death.
   4. The leadership level of the world is in jeopardy with such a competition of a life-changing message.
   5. The anti-Christs are on notice with a threat of the Gospel rising in these last days.

D. The line has been drawn to be on one side or the other.
   - Luke 11:23, "He that is <u>not with me</u> is <u>against me</u>: and he that <u>gathereth</u> not with me <u>scattereth</u>."

➤ The Valley of Elah had the armies of Israel on one side and an arrogant giant of the Philistines on the other. The message was not cast or received until David showed up and defeated the enemy with these words; "…but I come to thee in the name of the Lord of hosts, the God of the armies of Israel, whom thou hast defied." I Samuel 17:45

- David was able to slay the impenetrable force that all had not attempted to try.
- The enemy smoke-screened with threats and intimidation that could not stand in real spiritual battle.

E. The enemy is nothing without followers to support his agenda, but all are nothing in the face of Almighty God. The devil will always deceive to the end.

- Revelation 20:7-10, "And when the thousand years are expired, Satan shall be loosed out of his prison, And shall go out to <u>deceive the nations</u> which are in the <u>four quarters of the earth</u>, Gog and Magog, to <u>gather them together to battle</u>: the <u>number of whom is as the sand of the sea</u>. And they went up on the breadth of the earth, and <u>compassed the camp of the saints about</u>, and the <u>beloved city</u>: and fire came down from God out of heaven, and <u>devoured them</u>. And the <u>devil that deceived them was cast into the lake of fire and brimstone</u>, where the beast and the false prophet are, and shall be tormented day and night for ever and ever."

The tragic end of society and every person that follows the path of the enemy will result in death. "There is a way which seemeth right unto a man, but the end thereof are the ways of death." Proverbs 14:12

F. The enemy will offer people promises that appeal to the flesh with no spiritual value. He tried this persuasion on Jesus while fasting in the desert.

- Matthew 4:1-4, "Then was Jesus led up of the Spirit into the wilderness to be <u>tempted of the devil</u>. And when he had fasted forty days and forty nights, he was afterward an hungered. And when the tempter came to him, he said, <u>If thou</u> <u>be the Son of God</u>, command that these stones be made bread. But he answered and said, <u>It is written</u>, <u>Man</u> shall not <u>live</u> by bread alone, but by every <u>word</u> that <u>proceedeth out of the mouth of God</u>." Jesus' deity, including setting Him on a pinnacle in Jerusalem (Vs 5), and taking Him on a high mountain (Vs 8) ; he offers Jesus the world.
- Matthew 4:9-10; "And saith unto him, All these things will I give thee, if thou wilt fall down and worship me. Then saith Jesus unto him, Get thee hence, Satan: for it is written, Thou shalt worship the Lord thy God, and him only shalt thou serve."
  1. Satan owns nothing, and can't give you anything but empty promises if you listen to him.
  2. God gives the orders, and He is the only one worth worshipping because Satan has no deity, as he pretends to have.
  3. The attributes of Satan's character are the only things he will give you. And the main one that he is guilty of is PRIDE. "Pride goeth before destruction, and an haughty spirit before a fall." Proverbs 16:18

G. The road to serving God leads to eternal success, as the road to serving Satan leads to a waste of time and destruction.
- I John 2:16-17, "For all that is in the world, the lust of the flesh, and the lust of the eyes, and the pride of life, is not of the Father, but is of the world. And the world passeth away, and the lust thereof: but he that doeth the will of God abideth for ever."

H. Obedience is the only course for victory. To stay focused on God's purpose is the task and the duty at hand, and is achievable.
- II Corinthians 10:3-6, "For though we walk in the flesh, we do not war after the flesh: (For the weapons of our warfare are not carnal, but mighty through God to the pulling down of strong holds;) Casting down imaginations, and every high thing that exalteth itself against the knowledge of God, and bringing into captivity every thought to the obedience of Christ; And having in a readiness to revenge all disobedience, when your obedience is fulfilled."

Remember that God will never lead us without the Holy Spirit, to go into a world that needs rescued from the enemy.

"But the anointing which ye have received of him abideth in you, and ye need not that any man teach you: but as the same anointing teacheth you of all things, and is truth, and is no lie, and even as it hath taught you, ye shall abide in him." I John 2:27

TEST YOUR KNOWLEDGE
SECTION VII

1. The Great Commission has a striking parallel to what Old Testament book? _____
2. Complete this verse found in Joshua 1:9 – "Have I not _____ _____? Be _____ and of a _____ _____; be not _____, neither be thou _____: for the Lord thy God is _____ _____ whithersoever thou goest."
3. When God's people march over the earth with the Gospel, His presence is a promise. True _____ False _____
4. The enemy will pose resistance. He will:
   a. Catch you un_____
   b. Go for your w_____
   c. Make you, d_____ G_____ W_____
5. Power, fame, and fortune are among the temptations the devil will use to distract you. According to I John 2:16, what other warnings?
   a. Lust of the _____
   b. Lust of the _____
   c. Pride of _____
6. Complete this verse found in Romans 12:2 – "And be not _____ to this _____: but be ye _____ by the _____ of your _____, that ye may _____ what is that _____, and _____, and perfect, will of God."
7. Fear is inflated by the enemy to keep us from God's agenda. True _____ False _____
   Finish this acronym: F_____ E_____ A_____ R_____
8. There are only two natural fears for the human being:
   a. The fear of _____

b. The fear of _____ _____

9. Complete this verse found in Matthew 10:28 – "And _____ _____ them which _____ the body, but are _____ _____ to kill the _____: but rather _____ him which is able to _____ both _____ and _____ in _____."

10. Jesus said to go and take up my cross. True _____ False _____

11. Complete this verse found in Matthew 16:24 – "Then said Jesus unto his disciples, If any man will come after me, let him _____ _____, and _____ _____ _____, and follow me."

12. The message of the cross has at least five things no other message has. Name them:
    a. E_____ R_____
    b. A S_____ F_____
    c. A S_____ C_____
       P_____
    d. A L_____ M_____
       P_____
    e. A T_____ E_____

13. The message of the enemy has no spiritual value; his message always appeals to the _____.

14. Complete these verses found in II Corinthians 10:3-6 – "For though we _____ in the _____, we do not _____ after the _____: (For the _____ of our _____ are not _____, but _____ through _____ to the pulling down of _____ _____;) Casting down _____ and every _____ _____ that _____ itself against the knowledge of God, and _____ into _____ every thought to the obedience of Christ; And having in a _____ to _____ _____ _____, when your obedience is fulfilled."

Many are Called, Few Chosen

SECTION VIII

God's Selective Service

- ❖ **His Choice**
- ❖ **The Life Plan**
- ❖ **The Evangelist is a Soul-Winner**
- ❖ **Staff Evangelists Needed**

I. Nobody Can Instruct God on Who to Choose
   A. Would you take the same wage for eleven hours of work as some would get for one hour of work? Yes__ No__

   B. Jesus told a parable in Matthew chapter 20 of the "Labourers in the Vineyard," in Matthew 20:1-16. Verses 1-2 state that the kingdom of Heaven is like unto a householder that went out early in the morning to hire labourers, and they all agreed to a penny. Verses 3-10 state that the owner chose more on the third hour to work, the sixth hour, the ninth hour, and the eleventh hour; all received a penny.
   - Matthew 20:11-12, "And when they had <u>received</u> it, they <u>murmured against the goodman</u> of the house, Saying, These <u>last have wrought but one hour</u>, and thou hast made them <u>equal</u> unto us, which have borne the burden and heat of the day." All agreed to a penny for working in the householder's vineyard; so what is the conflict about?

- Matthew 20: 15-16; "Is it not lawful for me to do what I will with mine own? Is thine eye evil, because I am good? So the last shall be first, and the first last: for many be called, but few chosen."

Will you serve yourself or will you serve God on his terms?

The Life Plan

Life is Uncertain

❖ Will God Choose Me?

II. My Life Plan
    A. Things in life don't always go as planned, therefore a domino effect happens as a result.
      1. The perfect plan of God in everyone's life rarely gets fulfilled.
      2. God can see where things of life and the world have gone awry, and He keeps the plan on course.
    B. Why does God choose certain people over others to do specific duties?
- I Corinthians 1:26-29, "For ye see <u>your calling,</u> brethren, how that not many <u>wise men</u> after the <u>flesh</u>, not many <u>mighty</u>, not many <u>noble</u>, are <u>called</u>: But God hath <u>chosen the foolish</u> things of the world to <u>confound the wise</u>; and God hath chosen the <u>weak things</u> of the world to <u>confound</u> the things which are mighty; And base things of the world, and things which are <u>despised</u>, hath God chosen, yea, and things which are not, to bring to nought things that are: That no flesh should glory in his presence." Many examples in the Bible pertain to such; like David, Gideon, etc., but there is a mystery to his sovereignty.
      1. Many can't see the big picture because their individual needs come first.
      2. Many think because they are important, He will choose them.

C. Jacob blessed his sons before he died, but oddly, he prophesied of their lives and their descendants and their purpose on this earth. God gave him insight.
D. Jonah was selected to carry out God's purpose, but was in total defiance.
   1. Jonah knew the mercy of God would give Nineveh a chance to repent. (Jonah 4:2)
   2. Jonah could see the big picture and fled.
E. Saul of Tarsus was a dangerous individual and sought to persecute Christians.
   1. He had a misdirected zeal.
   2. He went out to set the world straight.
   "And Saul, yet breathing out threatenings and slaughter against the disciples of the Lord, went unto the high priest." Act 9:1
F. God's divine plan deals with Salvation. Those who can see the "big picture," the worldwide condition of people; God will choose to carry out His purpose.
   1. After Paul's eyes were opened, he was humbled to Christ's plan. "And he trembling and astonished said, Lord, what wilt thou have me to do?" (Acts 1:6)
   2. David humbled his heart and declared in Psalm 8: 3-4, "When I consider thy heavens, the work of thy fingers, the moon and the stars, which thou hast ordained; What is man, that thou art mindful of him? and the son of man, that thou visitest him?"

The Evangelist is a Soul-Winner

Evangelize to Win

III. The Evangelist is Committed to Win
    A. The Olympian will train to be the best as the Evangelist will never stop renewing his endurance.
- Romans 12:2, "And be not <u>conformed to this world</u>: but be ye <u>transformed by the renewing of your min</u>d, that ye may <u>prove</u> what is that good, and acceptable, and perfect, will of God." The evangelist will not be satisfied as the common Christian that merely goes through the motions.
    1. It is more than repetition of passing out tracts, etc. as others do.
    2. Looking for better ways to reach the lost is a challenge to achieve.
    B. There are three levels of people willing to evangelize:
1. Level One – The witness, who will share their faith and invite people to church.
2. Level Two – The Soul-Winner, who will share their faith and be determined to lead someone to Christ.
3. Level Three – The soul-Winner, who is determined to win people to Christ; who are fearless, fire-breathing, Spirit-led, individuals, who want to impact the world for Christ.

    C. The level three Soul-Winner is in a category all by himself; the term should be more correct in naming him a "Soul-Warrior," as in Hebrews 11.

- Hebrews 11:36-40; "And <u>others had trial of cruel mockings and scourgings, yea, moreover of bonds and imprisonment:</u> They were <u>stoned</u>, they were <u>sawn asunder</u>, were <u>tempted</u>, were <u>slain</u> with the sword: they <u>wandered about</u> in sheepskins and goatskins; being <u>destitute, afflicted, tormented</u>; (<u>Of whom the world was not worthy</u>:) they <u>wandered</u> in deserts, and in mountains, and in dens and caves of the earth. And these all, having obtained a <u>good report through faith</u>, <u>received not the promise</u>: God having provided <u>some better thing</u> for us, that they without us should not be made perfect."

This kind of person served God and never saw earthly rewards, but followed God for Heavenly rewards. Missionaries would fall in this category because of their unstoppable drive to change the world for Jesus Christ.

D. The Soul-Warrior is an individual that is well needed in our churches today, to take the lead in evangelism and impact the community.
E. Evangelism is being neglected in churches today resulting in no "New Life" to lift the many souls of our Pastors and members.
F. There are two main reasons that people don't go to church:
  1. Boring – can't understand the Word being preached.
  2. Irrelevant – what difference does it make anyways.
G. A fresh purpose is needed and people need to see a fresh-fire from God, so to say, that lives

are being changed and unique joy is being shared, and faith is being strengthened.

Staff Evangelist Needed

Dedicated to the Great Commission

IV. The Staff Evangelist is needed today.
   A. Every New Testament, Bible believing church needs an Evangelist.
      1. Whether paid staff or volunteer, this leader is necessary.
      2. This is not the Pastor, who equips the saints; he is over-seer and shepherd.
   B. This person is a Soul-Warrior armed with the Word of God and the Whole Armor of God.
      1. He has a burden for lost souls.
      2. He has to be in a church where the focus is on Salvation.
   C. The Church should pray for a person who can fulfill this responsibility, because the Church:
      1. Is to advance – "…The gates of hell shall not prevail against it." (the church) Matthew 16:18
      2. Is ordained to fulfill the Great Commission – "Go ye into all the world, and preach the gospel to every creature." Mark 16:15
   D. Paul's charge to Timothy on this matter:
   - II Timothy 4:3-5, "For the <u>time will come</u> when they will not <u>endure sound doctrine</u>; but after their <u>own lusts</u> shall they heap to themselves <u>teachers</u>, having itching ears; And they shall <u>turn away their ears from the truth</u>, and shall be turned unto <u>fables</u>. But watch thou in all things, endure afflictions, do the <u>work of an evangelist</u>, make <u>full proof</u> of thy ministry."

      1. Paul knew that the day would come when the Church would try other methods of worship and leave out the truth.
      2. He charges Timothy to endure this form of apostasy and keep on track; stick to the God-called ministry.
  E. Many are called, but few are chosen to take this call as a priority.
      1. The love for people.
      2. A noticeable decline in souls being saved

Someone has to stand in the stream of an ever-flowing culture of unbelief and moral corruption.

"Looking for that blessed hope, and the glorious appearing of the great God and our Saviour Jesus Christ." Titus 2:13

TEST YOUR KNOWLEDGE
SECTION VIII

1. Would you take the same wage for eleven hours of work that some receive for one hour? Yes _____ No _____ Consider it is God that pays you.
2. Complete this verse found in Matthew 20:12 – "Saying, These _____ have wrought but _____ _____, and thou hast made them _____ unto us, which have _____ the _____ and heat of the day."
3. Many are called, but few are chosen.
   True _____ False _____
4. Why does God choose certain people over others?
   a. Many can't see the big picture because their needs come first. _____
   b. Many think because they are important, God will choose them. _____
   c. All the above. _____
5. Complete these verses found in I Corinthians 1:26-29 – "For ye see _____ _____, brethren, how that not many _____ _____ after the _____, not many _____, not many _____, are called: But God hath _____ the _____ things of the world to _____ the wise; and God hath chosen the _____ things of the world to _____ the things which are mighty; And _____ things of the world, and things which are _____, hath God chosen, yea, and things which are _____, to bring to _____ things that are: That no _____ should _____ in his presence."
6. To whom is this verse referring to? "And he trembling and astonished said, Lord, what wilt thou have me to do?"
   _____ Peter

_____ Paul
_____ Isaiah
_____ David
_____ Saul of Tarsus
7. The evangelist is committed, as the Olympian, to _____, and will not be _____ as the common Christian.
8. Complete this verse found in Romans 12:2 – "And be not _____ to this _____: but be ye _____ by the _____ of your _____, that ye may _____ what is that good, and acceptable, and _____, will of God."
9. There are three levels of people willing to evangelize. True ____ False ____
10. Match the level with the correct description:
   Level One _____
   Level Two _____
   Level Three _____
   a. The Soul-Winner will share their faith, and be determined to lead someone to Christ.
   b. The Witness will share their faith and invite someone to church.
   c. The Soul-winner that is determined to win people to Christ; who is a fearless, fire-breathing, Spirit-led, individual, who wants to impact the world for Christ.
11. The Missionaries committed to their field have laid down their lives for the Gospel; the committed Soul-Winner, like the Missionary, could be called a: "S_____ W_____."
12. Churches need Soul-Warriors today to ensure that Salvation stays a main priority. The person to lead this ministry in the Church is called a "S_____ E_____."
13. This Ministry should not be the Pastor, but approved by him. The Pastor still has to be the person that:

a. Equips the S_____, to live faithfully to God.
b. Be an O_____, of all church ministries and activities.
c. The S_____, who protects and rescues the flock.

14. Complete these verses found in II Timothy 4:3-5 – "For the _____ will come when they will not _____ _____ _____; but after their _____ _____ shall they _____ to themselves _____, having itching ears; And they shall _____ _____ their ears from the _____, and shall be turned unto _____. But _____ thou in all things, _____ _____, do the work of an _____, make _____ _____ of thy ministry."

15. The time has come when the prophetic predictions of the Church are upon us, therefore a S_____ E_____ is needed to help with the Pastor.
True _____ False _____

The Soul Patrol

SECTION IX
Can You Work Alone? – Teamwork
- ❖ **The Spirit is Willing**
- ❖ **Keep the Call and Vision Alive**
- ❖ **Territory**
- ❖ **Soul Patrol**

I. Can a Person be Too Busy? The Spirit is Willing.

1. Responsibilities mount up over time and you can keep adding them on until you break.
2. Moses had tenacity and courage, but overlooked the load.
   - Exodus 18:13-18, "And it came to pass on the morrow, that Moses sat to judge the people: and the <u>people stood by Moses from the morning to the evening</u>. And when Moses' father in law saw all that he <u>did to the people</u>, he said, What is this thing that thou doest to the people? why sittest thou thyself <u>alone</u>, and all the people stand by thee from morning unto even? And Moses said unto his father in law, Because the people <u>come unto me to enquire of God</u>: When they have a matter, they come unto me; and I judge between one and another, and I do make them know the statutes of God, and his laws. And Moses' father in law said unto him, The thing that thou doest <u>is not good</u>. <u>Thou wilt surely wear away</u>, both thou, and this <u>people</u> that is with thee: for this thing is <u>too heavy for</u>

thee: <u>thou art not able to perform</u> it thyself alone."

Burn-out was in Moses' future if he continued serving God in this capacity.

3. God called Moses to lead a massive amount of people, but was he the only one capable to listen and counsel?
4. The people had disputes that started with two, then multiplied to six, eight, etc., and accumulated way out of proportion.
5. Can a person serve God with joy from the Holy Spirit when:
    - Over worked – the load is too much?
    - Misplaced – doesn't have the Spiritual Gift for the task?
6. Can a person effectively fulfill their calling when distracted with responsibilities that others should be doing? This will affect his walk and faith.
    - James 1:8, "A double minded man is unstable in all his ways."
7. The "main thing" needs to stay the "main thing." We can be drained of our wisdom and time otherwise. Exodus 18:21, "Moreover thou shalt provide out of all the people able men, such as fear God, men of truth, hating covetousness; and place such over them, to be rulers of thousands, rulers of hundreds, rulers of fifties, and rulers of tens."

Keeping the Call and Vision Alive
Salvation is Priority

II. Keeping the Call and Vision Alive is the Biggest Challenge
   A. The Evangelist is wise, but he is called for leadership in Salvation – "Salvation First," to be "Fishers of Men," "We catch them, God will clean them."
   B. Moses delivered the children of Israel, but Aaron was in the position of a priest.
   C. There stands an uncertain notion-- if God meant for Moses to go into the Promised Land or not.

   Closer Look

   1. Moses disobeyed God and was not allowed in – Moses' weakness.
   2. Moses' bold statement; "Fear ye not, stand still, and see the salvation of the Lord, which he will shew to you to day." Exodus 14:13 - The Evangelist's job is to lead others to Salvation.
   3. God knew this imperfect, at first reluctant, servant could be used to carry out His message and deliverance. A deliverer indeed.

   D. He did not accomplish all of this alone.
   Teamwork is required to win the lost to Christ.
   1. Heaven is our destination, as the Promised Land.
   2. The multitudes need leadership.

3. Similar to the counselling sessions, the troops have to be taught and guided to prepare for battle.
E. The big challenge is to find the ones who will answer the call of winning the lost souls for Christ, then:
 1. The Pastor needs to give the Evangelist/Soul-Warrior time and opportunity to preach.
 2. Help cast the Vision for new heavenly arrivals; "Where there is no vision, the people perish…" Proverbs 29:18
 3. Pray earnestly; "The effectual fervent prayer of a righteous man availeth much." James 5:16
 4. Once people see spiritual victories, curiosity arises in their heart and God changes them. It has been said, "this ministry is not taught, but caught." The Holy Spirit makes you a student.
F. Again, this ministry is not the responsibility of the Pastor directly. He has a calling for equipping the Saints and Church Administration under Pastor/Teacher.
 - Ephesians 4:11-12, "And he gave some, apostles; and some, prophets; and some, evangelists; and some, pastors and teachers; For the perfecting of the saints, for the work of the ministry, for edifying the body of Christ."

 The Pastor would be over- burdened and feeling guilty for not giving Evangelism his full, undivided attention.
G. Organize for success by casting this Heavenly Vision. The Mission.

- John 4:34-38, "Jesus saith unto them, My meat is to do the will of him that sent me, and to finish his work. Say not ye, There are yet four months, and then cometh harvest? behold, I say unto you, Lift up your eyes, and look on the fields; for they are white already to harvest. And he that reapeth receiveth wages, and gathereth fruit unto life eternal: that both he that soweth and he that reapeth may rejoice together. And herein is that saying true, One soweth, and another reapeth. I sent you to reap that whereon ye bestowed no labour: other men laboured, and ye are entered into their labours."
- John 3:3, "…Verily, verily, I say unto thee, Except a man be born again, he cannot see the kingdom of God."

Territory

Claim the Land

III. The Earth is Our Territory.
   A. Who owns the ground we are attempting to claim for Jesus Christ?

   - Psalm 24:1, "The <u>earth is the Lord's</u>, and the <u>fulness thereof</u>; the <u>world,</u> and <u>they</u> that dwell therein."

   1. Satan thinks he does, and we are trespassing.
   2. His followers are blinded and believe they have some power.
   3. In reality, Almighty God owns it all.

   B. In an airplane, you can see the boundaries of the towns and cities, and get a picture of what Satan and his demons are claiming.
   C. Let the Prince of the Power of the Air think that he controls and influences everyone.

   - Matthew 13:24-25, "Another parable put he forth unto them, saying, The kingdom of heaven is likened unto a man which <u>sowed good seed</u> in his field: But while men slept, his enemy came and <u>sowed tares</u> among the wheat, and went his way." The enemy will never cease sowing tares, but the Christians can't cease sowing either.
   - Matthew 13:30, "Let both <u>grow together</u> until the <u>harvest</u>: and in the <u>time of harvest</u> I will say to the reapers, Gather ye together <u>first the tares</u>, and <u>bind them in bundles to burn</u> them: but gather the <u>wheat into my barn</u>."

           1. We are to sow the seed among the tares.
           2. We are to reap the harvest when we can, and God will do the rest at judgment.
        D. What are some obvious tares?
           1. False Religions; Mosques, Temples, Shrines, etc. have become accepted across the USA and the world. "Get thee hence, Satan: for it is written, Thou shalt <u>worship</u> <u>the Lord thy God</u>, and him <u>only</u> shalt thou serve." Matthew 4:10
           2. Riches and Power; "For the <u>love of money</u> is the root of all evil: which while some <u>coveted after</u>, they have <u>erred from the faith</u>, and <u>pierced</u> themselves through with many <u>sorrows</u>." I Timothy 6:10. Lives have been ruined by the lust and greed of money throughout history, and this tare reaches into the very soul of a person, lost or saved.

Soul Patrol

Keeping an Eye on Things

IV. The Soul Patrol is on Duty.
- The world is infiltrated with Satan's accomplishments, and no one man can stop this advancement.
- It is time to group messengers with the Word of God and the saving knowledge of the Lord Jesus Christ.
- Precious Souls are at stake and they need to be reached before the enemy destroys them.
    - Matthew 28:18-20, "<u>All power is given unto me in heaven and in earth. Go ye therefore, and teach all nations</u>, baptizing them in the name of the Father, and of the Son, and of the Holy Ghost: Teaching them to observe all things whatsoever I have commanded you: and, lo, I am with you alway, even unto the end of the world. Amen."
- Jesus said to His disciples in Matthew 4:19, "Follow me, and I will make you fishers of men."
    1. The world is like a great sea of people that are dear and precious to God.
    2. Evangelism is not a passive approach nor a lifestyle type example, but an aggressive planned out mission.
- The new group of Soul-Winners need to be aggressive.
    1. People move in and out of neighborhoods and towns continuously.

2. Surroundings change, such as cars, homes, etc. As a policeman would patrol, he notices changes.
  3. New prospects arise, and someone needs to be watching and praying for God to show them who needs Salvation.
- The Soul-Warrior, as the leader, needs to lead with strategy and plan meetings to give confidence to this new group, keeping the purpose on track.
- The leader will divide areas to evangelize, from local neighborhood, to nearby towns, to major cities, using forms of reaching people such as:
  1. Busy places to hand out tracts – seeds are sown.
  2. Door to door – breakthroughs with politeness.
  3. Social media – the only way some will respond.
  4. Invite to special events – planned out for Salvation.

Keep in mind that the field is already ripe, as Jesus said, because God has already been working on hearts.

- Essentials of the Soul Patrol:
  1. People are lost and we know the way. Matthew 9:36-38
     a. They have no shepherd. – Vs.36
     b. Who will care as Jesus does. – Vs.36
     c. Your challenge is clear. – Vs.37
     d. The harvest belongs to Jesus. – Vs.38
  2. Our humility is needed every time. James 4:10

       a. Jesus had humility to the Father. Luke 22:42
       b. Paul's humility to become all things to all men. I Cor. 9:22
       c. Weakness will become strength. II Cor. 12:10
3. Obedience is required. Isaiah 6:8-10
       a. Nobody gets saved without going out or putting forth an effort. Rom. 10:17
       b. The Holy Spirit helps you yield. II Cor. 1:22, Rom. 6:19
4. Go believing. Rom. 1:16, Psa. 126:6

Every time we lead someone to the Lord, we will experience a heavenly joy beyond compare. The Lord will touch you deeply with a spiritual sense of feeling the love as he has. Then our Spiritual growth leaps in all areas because our desire to be close and walk with God deepens. "Our Greatest Opportunity" has become a whole-hearted commitment and dedication to Almighty God – Win the Victory!

TEST YOUR KNOWLEDGE
SECTION IX

1. Can a person be too busy serving God? Yes _____ No_____
2. Moses judged and counselled the children of Israel from morning to evening. True _____ False_____
3. Complete these verses found in Exodus 18:17-18 – "And Moses' father in law said unto him, The _____ that thou _____ is _____ _____. Thou wilt surely _____ _____, both _____, and _____ _____ that is with thee: for this thing is _____ _____ for thee: thou art not _____ to perform it _____ _____."
4. The "main thing" needs to stay the "_____ _____."
5. A person cannot accomplish a Soul-Winning Evangelistic Ministry alone; the biggest challenge is to: (check one)
   a. Give money to support the ministry. _____
   b. Find those who will answer the call. _____
   c. Invite people to church. _____
6. Complete these verses found in Ephesians 4:11-12 – "And he gave some, _____; and some, _____; and some, _____; and some, _____ and _____; For the _____ of the _____, for the work of the ministry, for the _____ of the body of Christ."
7. Satan thinks he owns the territory of planet earth, and the Evangelist is T_____.
8. The enemy will sow tares among the wheat according to Matthew 13:25. What are some obvious tares sown?
   a. False Religions _____

b. Riches _____
   c. Power _____
   d. All the above _____
9. Evangelism is not a passive approach or a lifestyle type example, but an _____ _____ _____ _____.
10. Complete these verses found in Matthew 28:18-20 – "And Jesus came and spake unto them, saying, _____ _____ is given unto me in _____ and in _____. _____ _____ therefore, and _____ all _____, baptizing them in the name of the _____, and of the _____, and of the _____ _____: Teaching them to observe all things whatsoever I have _____ _____: and, lo, I am with you _____, even unto the end of the world."
11. Four essentials of the "Soul Patrol" are:
    a. P_____ are lost and we k_____ the w_____.
    b. Our h_____ is needed every time.
    c. O_____ is required.
    d. Go b_____.
12. Every time we lead someone to the Lord, we will experience a h_____ j_____ beyond compare. The Lord will t_____ you d_____ with a spiritual sense of l_____ as he has.

The Lordship of Jesus Christ

SECTION X

The Lord of All
- ❖ **The Name of Jesus**
- ❖ **Our Personal Commission and Charter**
- ❖ **Jesus Owns it All**
- ❖ **In Reverence and Propagation of Salvation**

  I. The Name of Jesus
   A. The name of Jesus is lifted in Worship with songs and testimonies to an exalted level.
   B. You don't serve the Church, you serve God, in the name of Jesus Christ.
   - Philippians 2:9-13, "Wherefore <u>God</u> also hath <u>highly exalted him</u>, and given him a <u>name which is above every name</u>: That at the <u>name of Jesus</u> <u>every knee should bow</u>, of things in heaven, and things in earth, and things under the earth; And that <u>every tongue should confess that Jesus</u> <u>Christ is Lord</u>, to the glory of the Father. Wherefore, my beloved, as ye have always obeyed, not as in my presence only, but now much more in my absence, <u>work out your own salvation with fear and trembling</u>. For it is <u>God which worketh in you</u> both to will and to do <u>his good pleasure</u>."
   C. Beyond the church walls, the name of Jesus still has power in you.
     1. Can He penetrate your heart, soul, and mind?

  2. To work out your "own Salvation," or mature as he told the Philippian church.
 D. Remember that Jesus has all power:
  1. Over Nature – all earthly elements, weather, water, food, etc. Mark 4:41
  2. Over Demons – "Hold thy peace, and come out of him." Luke 4:35
  3. Over Death and Hell – "I am he that liveth, and was dead; and, behold, I am alive for evermore, Amen; and have the keys of hell and of death." Rev. 1:18
 E. He can work in you over your issues because you are a big part of the equation.
- I John 4:3-4, "And <u>every spirit that confesseth not that Jesus Christ is come in the flesh is not of God: and this is that spirit of antichrist</u>, whereof ye have heard that it should come; and even <u>now already</u> is it in the <u>world</u>. <u>Ye are of God,</u> little children, and <u>have overcome them</u>: because <u>greater</u> is <u>he that is in you,</u> than <u>he that is in the world</u>."

 F. When Satan was bound to the second heaven, he became:
  1. The single most deterrent for people to accept Christ, with nothing real to offer.
  2. The tempter will lure the Christian back to an ungodly life, just by playing on our weaknesses.
- Ephesians 6:12, "For we <u>wrestle not</u> against flesh and blood, but against <u>principalities</u>, against <u>powers</u>, against the <u>rulers of the darkness</u> of this world, against <u>spiritual wickedness</u> in high places."

Our Personal Commission and Charter

Salvation is His Will

II. Our Personal Commission and Charter
A. We are chosen to do His will.

Ephesians 1:4-5, "According as <u>he hath chosen us in him</u> before the <u>foundation of the world</u>, that we should be <u>holy and without blame</u> before him in <u>love</u>: Having <u>predestinated us</u> into the adoption of children by Jesus Christ to himself, according to the <u>good pleasure of his will</u>."

This means that we are chosen in His will to do His will.
B. What is His will?
1. To present Salvation – the generational cycle never stops.
2. To change people's lives – Starting at Salvation and a continual growth process.
3. "Be ye Holy," or separate, leaving worldliness behind and focusing on the Divine purpose.

C. Our field is a fallen, cursed world, in a realm of non-spiritual (ungodly) territory that is as dense as gravity, pulling every soul down.

D. Man has a free will to decide to follow Jesus or some kind of religion that falls short of the glory of God.

1. We have people who go to worship God, some get saved.
2. Some will pray to keep the soul clean.
3. Some will engage in the battle safely behind the trenches.
4. All will practice living in deception that there is a safe boundary from the enemy. This is non-existent, only pure deception.

"But be ye <u>doers of the word</u>, and <u>not hearers only</u>, <u>deceiving your</u> <u>own selves</u>. For if any be a <u>hearer of the word</u>, and not a <u>doer</u>, he is like unto a man <u>beholding</u> his <u>natural face in a glass</u>: For he beholdeth himself, and goeth his way, and straightway <u>forgetteth</u> what manner of <u>man he was</u>."
Jam. 1:22-24

Jesus Owns it All

Where do You Stand?

    III.   Jesus Has Always Owned it All.
- A. Jesus is the owner, the devil thinks that he is, and the battle is raging.
- B. Either you are pushing forward or you are slipping back with the rest of the world.
  - Matthew 12:30, "He that is not <u>with me is against me</u>; and he that gathereth not with me scattereth abroad."
- C. The main question is, how long can people stay lukewarm? There is no neutrality.
  - Revelation 3:17, "Because thou sayest, <u>I am rich</u>, and increased with goods, and have <u>need of nothing</u>; and knowest not that thou are <u>wretched</u>, and miserable, and <u>poor</u>, and <u>blind,</u> and <u>naked</u>."
  - Revelation 3:22, "He that hath an ear, let him hear what the <u>Spirit saith unto the churches</u>."
- D. Does Jesus judge churches today, as in the seven churches of Asia? Many will come up short because of the enemies' vain imagination.
  - Psalm 2:1-4, "Why do the <u>heathen rage</u>, and the <u>people imagine a vain thing</u>? The <u>kings</u> of the earth <u>set themselves</u>, and the <u>rulers take counsel together</u>, <u>against the Lord</u>, and against <u>his anointed</u>, saying, Let us <u>break their</u>

bands asunder, and cast away their cords from us. He that sitteth in the heavens shall laugh: the Lord shall have them in derision." "*derision*;" to stammer

   E. The devil and those who follow him have in mind to break the Christian purpose and to win the Spiritual battle by joining forces and showing earth a better way.

   F. Jesus is the only "way, the truth, and the life." John 14:6
      1. The Way – to Heaven and true spirituality.
      2. The Truth – not a deceptive and false picture of hope.
      3. The Life – eternal, that starts for us at conversion and we take the position with Jesus on the platform of Victory.

   G. If God be for us, who can stand against us? Jesus is the anointed of God and the preeminent leader.

- Isaiah 11:1-4, "And there shall come forth a rod out of the stem of Jesse, and a Branch shall grow out of his roots: And the spirit of the Lord shall rest upon him, the spirit of wisdom and understanding, the spirit of counsel and might, the spirit of knowledge and of the fear of the Lord; And shall make him of quick understanding in the fear of the Lord: and he shall not judge after the sight of his eyes, neither reprove after the hearing of his ears: But with righteousness shall he judge the poor, and reprove with equity for the meek of the earth: and he shall smite the earth with the rod of his mouth,

and with the breath of <u>his lips shall he slay the wicked</u>."
1. He will be the one standing in the clouds at rapture before the Great Tribulation.
2. He will lead the charge with ten thousands of His saints at Armageddon.
3. He will lead with a rod of iron in the Millennial Kingdom.
4. The one that all Christians will serve for all eternity after he judges the world.
5. He will have the last say, of the history of the entire world; all souls are in His hands.

In Reverence and Propagation of Salvation

This Do In Remembrance of Me

    IV. In Reverence of Jesus and Accepting His Charge for Salvation.
      A. Jesus stretched out His arms and was nailed to a cross, sacrificing His body and blood for our sins and eternal life.
      B. We can't put the blame on the regime of the day for His crucifixion; it was God's plan all along for Jesus to offer himself. He came to die that we may have life. (John 10)
      C. The Lord's Supper is a ceremony of the remembrance and of the propagation of eternal life.
      D. Each New Testament Church practices this ceremony as a memorial service, but each should realize the true meaning of the sacrament.
      E. This service is a charge to the Saints to pass along a "communication," or "communion," of Jesus the Son, from God the Father, to us, the believers of eternal life.
      1. This service doesn't save you.
      2. This service reminds us of the power of one who can give us personal Salvation. "This do in remembrance of me..." (Luke 22, I Cor. 11), is the propagation of salvation, just as God told Adam and Eve to "Be fruitful, and multiply, and replenish the earth, and subdue it..." Gen. 1:28

F. There is no limit to how often the local church will need this recharge, but do not fail to educate the believers of its purpose.
   - I Corinthians 11:26, "For as often as ye eat this bread, and drink this cup, ye do shew the Lord's death till he come." As needed.
G. The Church has a high calling from God to hear His voice, to reach the lost for Jesus Christ now, for the kingdom of God is at hand.
   - Hebrews 12:23-29, "To the <u>general assembly and church of the firstborn, which are written in heaven</u>, and to God the Judge of <u>all,</u> and to the <u>spirits of just men made perfect</u>, And to Jesus the <u>mediator of the new covenant</u>, and to the <u>blood of sprinkling</u>, that speaketh <u>better things</u> than that of Abel. See that ye <u>refuse not him that speaketh</u>. For if they <u>escaped not</u> who refused him that spake on earth, <u>much more shalt not we escape</u>, if we turn away from him that <u>speaketh from heaven</u>: Whose voice then <u>shook the earth</u>: but now he hath <u>promised,</u> saying, Yet once more I <u>shake not the earth only</u>, but <u>also heaven</u>, And this word, yet once more, signifieth the <u>removing </u>of those things that are shaken, as of things that are made, that those things which <u>cannot be shaken may remain</u>. Wherefore we <u>receiving a kingdom which cannot be moved</u>, let us have <u>grace</u>, whereby we may <u>serve God acceptably with reverence and godly fear: For our God is a consuming fire</u>."
H. The invitation has been given out, but the commission continues until the house is full. As in the parable of the "Great Supper,"

many refused, but the commission remained. (Luke 14:16-24)

- Luke 14:23, "And the lord said unto the servant, <u>Go out into the highways and hedges, and compel them to come in, that my house may be filled</u>."

The very salvation of one soul will be determined by how the Church "compels" them to come in. The duel meaning is clear; compel into church and the kingdom of God.

TEST YOUR KNOWLEDGE
SECTION X

1. In the name of Jesus, every K_____ S_____ B_____.
2. "Work out your own Salvation" with fear and trembling means to:
   a. Continue working because you are saved _____
   b. To become mature _____
   c. Let God work in you _____
   d. Have humility in serving _____
   e. All the above _____
3. Jesus has power over:
   a. N_____ (Mark 4:41)
   b. D_____ (Luke 4:35)
   c. D_____ and H_____ (Rev. 1:18)
4. Satan is bound to the second heaven.
   True _____ False _____
5. Complete this verse found in Ephesians 6:12 – "For we _____ not against _____ and _____, but against _____, against _____, against the _____ of the _____ of this _____, against _____ _____ in high places."
6. We are chosen to do God's will according to what verses in Ephesians? "…he hath chosen us in him" _____, and "predestinated us… for his good pleasure" _____
7. All Christians will experience a deception at some time, that there is a safe boundary from the enemy. This boundary is n____-_____ and p_____ d_____.

8. Complete these verses found in James 1:22-24 -- "But be ye _____ of the _____, and not _____ only, _____ your own selves. For if any be a _____ of the word and not a _____, he is like a man _____ his _____ _____ in a glass: For he beholdeth himself, and _____ his way, and straightway _____ what _____ of man he _____."
9. Can a person stay in neutral and serve the Lord? Yes _____ No _____
10. Satan will recruit followers to join the Spiritual battle, because he wants to show earth a better way.
True _____ False _____
11. John 14:6 states that Jesus is the only: W_____, T_____, and L_____; therefore, we take position with Him on the platform of victory.
12. The Lord's Supper is not just a memorial service, but a charge to the Saints for the propagation of salvation.
True _____ False _____
13. As God told Adam and Eve to "Be fruitful, and multiply, and replenish the earth, and subdue it..." (Gen. 1:28), the charge is to the Christian the same.

True _____ False _____

14. Complete this verse found in Luke 14:23 – "And the lord said unto the _____, Go out into the _____ and _____, and _____ them to _____ _____, that my house may be filled."

Accepting Christ

SECTION XI
The Power of God's Word
- ❖ **A Sword and a Light**
- ❖ **Step it Up and Stand on the Rock**
- ❖ **Reformation or Transformation?**
- ❖ **Proof of Salvation**

I. The Word of God is a sharp sword and a light.
   A. Someone, somewhere, shared the Word of God with you before you got saved.
- Hebrews 4:12, "For the <u>word of God is quick</u>, and <u>powerful</u>, and <u>sharper</u> than any <u>twoedged sword</u>, <u>piercing</u> even to the <u>dividing asunder of soul and</u> <u>spirit</u>, and of the joints and marrow, and is a <u>discerner</u> of the <u>thoughts</u> and <u>intents of the heart</u>."
  1. You might have been stubborn and wouldn't listen.
  2. The devil might have had you in spiritual bondage.
  3. The exposure eventually pierced the walls of your heart.

   B. The more a person hears the true wisdom of God's Word, he or she is drawn in to an irresistible desire to accept counsel from it. When Hebrews 4:12 states that it is a "discerner of the thoughts and intents of the heart":
1. This counsel will continue your whole life.
2. This counsel will divide and cultivate into right thinking.
3. Help you make the right decisions to stand on.

C. Total understanding might be possible for all things, so the Holy Spirit assures you that you are on the right path.
- Psalms 119:105-107, "Thy <u>word</u> is a <u>lamp unto my feet</u>, and a <u>light unto</u> <u>my path</u>. I have <u>sworn,</u> and I will <u>perform</u> it, that I will <u>keep</u> thy <u>righteous judgments</u>. I am <u>afflicted</u> very much: <u>quicken me</u>, O Lord, <u>according unto</u> <u>thy word</u>."
- Psalm 119:130, "The <u>entrance</u> of thy words giveth <u>light</u>; it giveth <u>understanding</u> unto the simple."

D. Victory is seen in two ways at this point:

1. The acceptance of Jesus Christ as Savior by the Word and the Holy Spirit – "Behold, I stand at the door, and knock: if any man hear my voice, and open the door, I will come into him, and will sup with him, and he with me." Revelation 3:20

2. A thirst to let the Word change the life of the new believer – "Blessed are they which do hunger and thirst after righteousness: for they shall be filled." Matthew 5:6

F. **Saturation of the Bible Preached and taught is required. Not seen as much today in churches.**

1. We have limited services, therefore, exposure is limited.
2. We have hit and miss themes and topics without a long duration of learning. As a result: it can take years to achieve sold-out believers in your church.

G. The Spiritual battle for attendance is real, with the enemy having ten times as much exposure than churches.

H. The most recent polls list two reasons why people don't want to go to church:
   1. Church is boring – the world has become sensationalists.
   2. Church is irrelevant – how does it apply to me?

Step it Up and Stand on the Rock

Time to Take a Stand

I. Step Up and Take a Stand on the Solid Rock, Jesus Christ.
- A. Now is the time to compete in ways to capture people's attention and not compromise the Word preached.
    - II Timothy 4:2-5, "<u>Preach the word</u>; be <u>instant in season</u>, <u>out of season</u>; <u>reprove, rebuke, exhort with all longsuffering and doctrine</u>. For the <u>time will come</u> when they will not <u>endure sound doctrine</u>; but after their own <u>lusts</u> shall they heap to themselves teachers, having itching ears; And they shall turn away their ears from the <u>truth</u>, and shall be turned unto <u>fables</u>. But <u>watch</u> thou in all things, <u>endure afflictions, do the work of an evangelist, make full proof of thy ministry</u>."
- B. The battle for the soul has intensified:
    1. Teachers with a taste for popularity, corrupting the truth into stories.
    2. Churches not standing on the Rock, but compromised to shifting sand by omitting the truth.
- C. The ministerial format of a church has to change to a flow of:
    1. Evangelists on the streets and all social media engaging in relevant issues – Salvation.

2. The Church needs to be an inviting place of worship where people feel comfortable, and in balance with preaching.
3. The Clergy has the vision to perpetuate the cycle of Salvation to the Soul-Winner.
4. The discipleship programs and Bible studies are constant; the early Church met daily.

D. In these times, there are two questions that should be on everyone's mind:
1. When will Jesus return – rapture?
2. Who will be saved and go to Heaven?

E. Prophecy must come to pass, and we are living in it now.
- Proverbs 29:18, "Where there is no <u>vision, the people perish</u>: but he that keepeth the law, happy is he." The Hebrew and the 1611 AV translate as no "<u>prophetic vision</u>," the people perish. Not high idealism, but prophetic leading by Almighty God.

F. Man-made plans and strategies can be used by the enemy to a fleshly appeal, but a Godly structure is the law of God. "Save yourselves from this untoward generation." Acts 2:40
- Acts 2:41, "Then they that gladly <u>received his word</u> were baptized: and the same day there were added unto them about three thousand souls."

G. Peter's preaching at Pentecost began by announcing the prophetic words of the prophet Joel.
- Acts 2:17-21, "And it shall come to pass in *the last days*, saith God, I will <u>pour out of my Spirit</u> upon all flesh: and your sons and daughters shall <u>prophesy</u>, and your young men shall <u>see visions</u>, and your old

men shall <u>dream dreams</u>: And on my servants and on my handmaidens I will pour out in those days of my Spirit; and they shall prophesy: And I will shew <u>wonders in heaven</u> above, and <u>signs in the earth</u> beneath; <u>blood, and fire, and vapour of smoke</u>: <u>The sun shall be turned into darkness</u>, and <u>the moon</u> <u>into blood</u>, before that great and <u>notable day of the Lord</u> come: And it shall come to pass, that whosoever shall <u>call on the name of the Lord shall be</u> <u>saved</u>."

Joel's prophecy was happening at the day of Pentecost, and now we are living in the post-Pentecost era when the Holy Spirit indwells all believers. He does not separate times until the "notable day of the Lord come."

H. Is the priority of Salvation and conversion anywhere in society today, with all beautiful buildings and diverse religions?

Churches and Temples might transcend the mind, but can't transform the Soul.

Reformation or Transformation?

Transformation is the Work of God

I. Reformation to Church or Transformation to God?
   A. The excitement of a service with inspiration, emotion, assurance, and inherent standing, has to be awarded to people getting saved and baptized.
   B. Music and heart-tugging moments are needed in a church, but genuine conversion is enough to keep people coming back. Good ideas can't replace the genuine article.
   C. It takes a body of believers to demonstrate the true commission of the Lord Jesus.
   - Acts 2:42, "And they <u>continued steadfastly</u> in the apostles' <u>doctrine</u> and <u>fellowship</u>, and in breaking of bread, and in <u>prayers</u>."
   1. In doctrine – the death, burial, and resurrection.
   2. In fellowship – the model of sharing.
   3. In breaking of bread – enjoying unity.
   4. In prayers – forging the power of God.
   D. The public was in awe and wonder because lives were eternally transformed and given a new direction by the Holy Spirit of God in the early Church.
   - II Corinthians 5:17-18, "Therefore if <u>any man be in Christ</u>, he is a <u>new creature</u>: <u>old things are passed away</u>; behold, <u>all things are become new</u>. And <u>all things are of God</u>, who hath <u>reconciled us</u> to himself

by Jesus Christ, and hath given to us the <u>ministry of reconciliation</u>."
E. Easy believism is a lack of genuine conversion. Some will seemingly get saved, join the group, reform to the church ways, and soon they will drop out of the church.
F. Genuine transformation to the Lord Jesus Christ starts with genuine repentance, then regeneration lifts the load of sin, and the soul of the person is miraculously changed forever.
   1. The regeneration of the soul is the work of the Holy Spirit. "…Except a man be born of water and of the Spirit, he cannot enter into the kingdom of God. That which is born of the flesh is flesh; and that which is born of the Spirit is spirit." John 3:5-6
   2. The spirit of man has been supernaturally challenged by the Spirit of God indwelling the New Believer. "Now we have received, not the spirit of the world, but the spirit which is of God; that we might know the things that are freely given to us of God." I Cor. 2:12
   3. Heaven is promised and their name is written in the Lamb's book of life. "And there shall in no wise enter into it any thing that defileth, neither whatsoever worketh abomination, or maketh a lie: but they which are written in the Lamb's book of life." Rev. 21:27
G. The Church should be cautious to reconcile sinners to God, not try to reform and conform people to church methods, when that person is not saved. We have the ministry of reconciliation. (II Cor. 5:18)

1. People get saved through the Word of God with the Holy Spirit.
2. People get saved with fellowship and prayers.
3. People will be baptized and join the church when the focus is on salvation.

Proof of Salvation

Saved to Serve

I. Proof of Salvation Will Bring Purpose.
    A. No longer should man wander through life with no wisdom or direction once saved.
    B. Mankind is made for God's pleasure to serve Him and none other.
- Ephesians 2:10; "For we are <u>his workmanship</u>, created in Christ Jesus unto <u>good works</u>, which God hath before ordained that we should <u>walk in</u> <u>them</u>."

    C. When someone is the real, genuine, absolutely saved individual, the sense of self-definition starts to come over them and questions are asked:
    1. What is the will of God for my life?
    2. What is my Spiritual gift?
    3. How can I serve God effectively?
    D. The babe in Christ is starting to desire the meat. The challenge of evangelism should be introduced and shown to them.
- I Corinthians 3:9-11, "For we are <u>labourers together</u> with God: ye are <u>God's husbandry</u>, ye are <u>God's building</u>. According to the grace of God which is given unto me, as a <u>wise masterbuilder</u>, I have laid the foundation, and another buildeth thereon. But let every man take heed how he buildeth thereupon. <u>For other foundation can no man lay than that is laid, which is Jesus Christ</u>."

      1. The Senior Pastor will recognize the Spiritual growth of the person.
      2. The staff Evangelist will direct them into a service of courage and promise.
E. With Spiritual tenacity, the new Evangelist will take on the challenge and accept the Great Commission to reach the lost. Therefore, Go –
- Matthew 28:19-20, "<u>Go ye therefore</u>, and <u>teach all nations</u>, <u>baptizing</u> them in the name of the <u>Father</u>, and of the <u>Son</u>, and of the <u>Holy Ghost</u>: <u>Teaching them to observe all things whatsoever I have commanded you</u>: and, lo, I am with you alway, even unto the end of the world."

TEST YOUR KNOWLEDGE
SECTION XI

1. Complete this verse found in Hebrews 4:12 – "For the _____ of _____ is _____, and _____, and _____ than any twoedged _____, _____ even to the _____ _____ of _____ and _____, and of the _____ and _____, and is a discerner of the _____ and _____ of the heart."
2. The more a person is exposed to the Word of God; the stronger the desire to accept its counsel. True _____ False _____
3. The Word of God is also likened to a light. Write out Psalms 119:105;
   " _____
   _____."

Psalms 119:130;
" _____
_____ "

4. We get enough saturation from the Word of God in churches today. True ___ False _____
5. The battle for attendance in churches is a challenge. Name two reasons that people today have for not going to church:
   a. Church is _____ - The world has become sensationalists.
   b. Church is _____ - How does it apply to me?
6. The need for sound doctrine is needed more than ever in churches today. True _____ False _____

7. In times like these, there should be two questions on everyone's mind:
   a. When will J_____ R_____?
   b. Who will be S_____ and going to H_____?

8. Biblical prophecy must come to pass, not high idealism, but prophetic leading by A_____ G_____.

9. Peter began preaching at Pentecost quoting the prophet _____ in what scripture reference? Acts _____

10. The excitement of a service with inspiration, emotion, assurance, and inherent standing, has to be awarded to people getting S_____ and B_____.

11. Complete this verse found in II Corinthians 5:17 – "Therefore if any man be in _____, he is a _____ _____: old things are _____ _____; behold, all things are become _____."

12. The regeneration of the Soul is the work of the Holy Spirit. True____ False ____

13. Heaven is promised to the new believer because their name is written in the L_____ B_____ of L_____.

14. According to II Corinthians 5:18, we have the ministry of r_____.

15. The Church should be cautious to r_____ sinners to God, not to try to c_____ people to Church methods when that person is not saved.

16. Complete this verse found in Ephesians 2:10 – "For we are his _____, created in Christ Jesus unto _____ _____, which God hath before _____ that we should _____ in _____."

16. The church should introduce evangelism at some point to the new believer, as he desires the meat of the Word. True _____ False_____

17. Evangelism is a ministry with both:
    a. C_____
    b. P_____

18. The Pastor will recognize Spiritual growth in a person, where the S_____ E_____ will teach and prepare them for the challenge of the G_____ C_____.

Revival Comes With Salvation

SECTION XII
Spiritual Awakening
❖ **Signs of Revival**
❖ **Our Present Opportunity**
❖ **Keeping on Track**

I. Signs of Revival.
   Everyone agrees about the need for a Spiritual awakening.
   A. What is a Revival?
      1. Raising the dead, the uninspired Christian.
      2. Fire to come down from Heaven as Elijah at Mt. Carmel.
   B. The world needs a full-blown righteous Crusade. All the signs are present, according to "Christian History Magazine," with five elements:
      1. Awakenings are usually preceded by a time of spiritual depression, apathy and gross sin, in which a majority of nominal Christians are hardly different from the members of secular society, and churches seem to be asleep.
      2. An individual or small group of God's people become conscious of their sins and backslidden condition, and vow to forsake all that is displeasing to God.
      3. As some Christians begin to yearn for a manifestation of God's power, a leader or leaders arise with a prophetic insight into the causes and remedies of the problems, and a new awareness of the Holy and pure character of the Lord is present.

4. The awakenings of Christians occur. Many understand and take part in a higher spiritual life.
5. An awakening may be God's means of preparing and strengthening His people for future challenges and trials.

   All these characteristics describe today's society, no matter what country or culture you are from.

C. Leaders are quick to point out and give lectures and sermons on the climate of society, but rarely do you hear solutions.
   - Matthew 10:34, "Think not that I am come to send <u>peace on earth</u>: I came not to send peace, <u>but a sword</u>." Translated: the conflict can only be dealt with by a swift and powerful sword of the Lord; "Sword of the Spirit," which is the Word of God. *(hrema), to divide*
D. The sword is accompanied with the "helmet of Salvation;" *(pelikos)*
   - Ephesians 6:17-18, "And take the <u>helmet of salvation</u>, and the <u>sword</u> of the Spirit, which is the <u>word of God</u>: Praying always with all prayer and supplication in the Spirit, and <u>watching</u> thereunto with all perseverance and supplication for all saints."
E. The sword and the helmet are led by prayer. Prayer is the one thing churches across the globe agree on to be an imperative ingredient for revival.
F. Revival does not come by prayer alone, but by engaging God's plan and using faith.

1. God can bring revival if our faith is not dead. "Even so faith, if it hath not works, is dead, being alone." James 2:17
2. We can't lay it all on God when we have not done our part. "...I will shew thee my faith by my works." James 2:18

Our Present Opportunity

Broadcast the Good News

II. Our Present Opportunity is clear.
    A. Pastors will intentionally and prayerfully plan revivals to bring a blast of preaching for decisions.
        1. The real truth by unapologetic preaching is needed.
        2. Many churched do not have revival anymore to awaken their people.
        3. More social networking is required, in which our society today has a wealth to offer.
    B. Broadcasting has been a very successful tool for many decades. Radio and television take the lead. But the cost can be too much for smaller churches.
    C. Social media via internet and social networking has entered the field, and some have been wise to use these very efficient tools.
    D. The enemy has the same access, but the Christian has the advantage.
        1. Satan is the Prince of the power of the air (Eph. 2:2), hammering away at the truth, trying to control the technology.
        2. Evangelism has the promise from God. The gates of Hell shall not prevail against the Church. (Mat. 16:18)
    E. Be careful and precise on the message broadcasted. Salvation is the intended result.
        1. Grandstanding will lead to no Salvation results.

2. Foundational truths will lead to genuine conversion.
"I therefore so <u>run, not as uncertainly</u>; so fight I, not as one that beateth the <u>air</u>." In this case, it is literally the "air." I Cor. 9:26
F. God knows the fullness of times and the urgency of the day.
- Acts 17:29-31, "Forasmuch then as we are the offspring of God, we ought not to think that the Godhead is like unto gold, or silver, or stone, graven by art and man's device. And the <u>times of this ignorance God winked at; but now commandeth all men every where to repent</u>: Because he hath <u>appointed a day</u>, in which he will <u>judge the world</u> in righteousness by that man whom he hath ordained; whereof he hath given <u>assurance unto all men</u>, in that day he hath raised him from the dead."

G. Spiritual Revival by the Spiritual Power of the Holy Spirit and the witness of the Christian, using now-day technology can bring great success. If the churches would awaken to the possibilities:
1. What if the message of Salvation culminated across the land?
2. What if people everywhere were on their knees praying for results?
3. Would a combined effort of Bible-believing churches get the attention of the public?
4. What if the culture started to change for the Kingdom of God?

Keeping on Track

Stay on Course

III. Keeping on Track is a challenge.
    A. The course of this world is obvious, but the course for the witness of Christ is commissioned only by God.
    B. The early Church followed the commission with a small group to go into Jerusalem, and all Judea, and Samaria, and to the uttermost part of the earth. (Acts 1:8) A tall order for a small group, but the charge was made by Jesus.
- Matthew 13:31-32, "The kingdom of heaven is like to a <u>grain of</u> <u>mustard seed</u>, which a man took, and <u>sowed</u> in his field: Which indeed is the <u>least of all seeds</u>: but when it is <u>grown</u>, it is the <u>greatest</u> among herbs, and becometh a tree, so that the <u>birds of the air</u> come and <u>lodge</u> in the branches thereof."
  1. Each man symbolizes Christ.
  2. The field is the world.
  3. The seed is the Word of God.
  4. The tree is the Church.
  5. The branches are the growth of the Church.

    C. Early evangelism has spread like the mustard seed and grown into astounding proportions all over the world.
    D. The branches of this great tree have provided roosting places for the enemy to leer at a view of fruit to devour.

E. The parable of the mustard seed refers to the birds of the air lodging in the branches. These birds are of the same references as:
   1. Revelation 18:2, "...Every unclean and hateful bird."
   2. Jeremiah 5:27, "As a cage is full of birds, so are their houses full of deceit."
F. Every unsound doctrine taught is ripe fruit for the enemy, with his agents waiting for the unsuspecting individual to believe it.
G. What can the enemy do about genuine Salvation?
   1. This doctrine is eternal.
   2. This doctrine is implemented by the Holy Spirit.
      - "In whom ye also trusted, after that ye heard the word of truth, the gospel of your salvation: in whom also after that ye believed, ye were sealed with that holy Spirit of promise." Ephesians 1:13
H. Why do we need revival in the first place?
   1. Christians have let the enemy sway them from the truth.
   2. Ministers recognize that the Church is getting off track or course.
   3. Some have the intentions of leading the Church astray into a casual Christianity.
   4. The Souls of men, women, and children are at stake, while moving into a godless society and culture.

   "The fruit of the righteous is a tree of life; and he that winneth souls is wise."

   The "tree" is the fruit of the righteous and brings "life;" New Life in Jesus Christ!

I. Our "Greatest Opportunity" is the "Great Commission," to spread the Gospel and to change the world, offering eternal life, promised from Almighty God. Salvation is the most important reason God sent his son into the world to die for all mankind.
- **I Corinthians 3:11, "For other foundation can no man lay than that is laid, which is Jesus Christ."**

J. Churches are divided about the doctrine of Salvation, but all can claim Souls saved. Revival can start to spread across the world as the early Church, if a combined effort were to start with a communication to network the results to everyone in a celebration to share with each other.

Together We Can Change the Culture Back to Salvation!

TEST YOUR KNOWLEDGE
SECTION XII

1. The world is in need of a revival.
   True _____ False _____
2. Write out at least three signs that revival is needed today.
   a. _____
   _____
   b. _____
   _____
   c. _____
   _____
3. Complete this verse found in Matthew 10:34 – "Think not that I am come to send peace on the earth: I came not to send _____, but a _____."
4. Prayer is one thing that churches across the globe can agree upon to bring revival. But prayer alone doesn't bring revival. What are two other main ingredients?
   a. E_____ God's P_____.
   b. Using F_____.
5. Complete these verses found in James 2:17-18 – "Even so _____, if it hath not _____, is _____, being alone. Yea, a man may say, Thou hast _____, and I have _____: shew me thy faith without thy works, and I will shew thee my faith _____ _____ works."
6. Even though Satan is called the "prince of the power of the air," the Church has the advantage in evangelism because the "g_____ of H_____ shall not p_____ against the C_____.
7. "Spiritual Revival" can happen across the land if:
   a. Churches could c_____ e_____ to get the public's attention.

b. People would get on their k_____ in p_____ for results.
   c. Determine to change the c_____ for the Kingdom of God.
8. Possibilities for Revival have to start small like the comparison Jesus made about the Kingdom of Heaven. Like a g_____ of m_____ s_____.
9. Complete these verses found in Matthew 13:31-32 - "…The kingdom of heaven is like to a _____ of _____ _____, which a man took, and _____ in his _____: Which indeed is the _____ of all _____: but when it is _____, it is the _____ among herbs, and _____ a _____, so that the birds of the air can come and _____ in the _____ thereof."
10. Why can't the enemy do anything about genuine Salvation?
    a. This doctrine is E_____.
    b. This doctrine is implemented by the H_____ S_____.
11. Complete this verse found in Proverbs 11:30 – "The _____ of the _____ is a _____ of _____; and he that _____ _____ is _____."
12. The Christian's "Greatest Opportunity," besides personal Salvation, is the "G_____ C_____."
13. Divisions on the doctrine of salvation are obvious among our churches today, but a combined effort to change the culture and bring Revival is possible. Yes _____ No _____

OUR GREATEST OPPORTUNITY ANSWER KEY

SECTION I
1. b. 1/3
2. 52%
3. c. 14%
4. Teach, baptizing, Father, Son, Holy Ghost
5. False
6. Plan, Power, Purpose
7. 151,600
8. Lamb's, Book, Life
9. "The fruit of the righteous is a tree of life; and he that winneth souls is wise."
   "He that goeth forth and weepeth, bearing precious seed, shall doubtless come again with rejoicing, bringing his sheaves with him."
10. harvest, lift up your eyes, look upon, fields

SECTION II
1. Yes
2. mission
3. c. Salvation
4. form, godliness, denying, power
5. True
6. heart, foolishness, madness, depravity, evil, unbelief extortion and excess (name three)
7. heart, believeth, confession, salvation
8. True

SECTION III
1. whole armour of God
2. whole armour of God, able, stand, wiles

3. True
4. An ordained system of ideas, self-inclusive and harmonious
5. warreth entangle himself, chosen, soldier
6. Possess, Sanctify, Edify Christ
7. Apprehensive State, obedience, God
8. Spirit, Soul, Body
9. True
10. Adam, Eve
11. sin
12. heard, voice, afraid
13. God, your soul, your body
14. Yes
15. profited, gain, whole world, soul, exchange
16. Renew, God's Word
17. a. Spirit
18. knoweth, spirit, man, God knoweth, Spirit, God

SECTION IV

1. go, die
2. die, live again, appointed time
3. appointed time
4. Sheol
5. Hades, Gehennah
6. Hell, torments
7. Paradise
8. God, sin, life the way it is, controlling, Jesus and Heaven, about going to church, be saved
9. Fruit, righteous, winneth souls, wise
10. sown, places, sown
11. reapeth, fruit, life eternal, soweth, reapeth, rejoice
12. online, cinema, social media
13. 19, 20, 22, 23
14. c. all of the above

SECTION V

1. Past, Present, Future
2. True
3. new heaven, new earth, first, first, passed away
4. Birth, Growth, Maturity
5. False
6. that day, knoweth no man, Father only
7. flood, Noah
8. False
9. saw, wickedness, man, imagination, heart, evil continually
10. True
11. Rapture, Tribulation, Millennium
12. time, evil
13. fire
14. True
15. last time, antichrist, antichrists, last time

SECTION VI

1. miss the mark, offence with penalty
2. knoweth, good, doeth, not, sin
3. sin abounded, grace, much more
4. God forbid
5. Yes
6. a. The soul is eternal and will go to Heaven or Hell
7. Romans 6:23, Hebrews 9:27
8. Christians exist here, none in Hell, I can quench my thirst here, not in Hell, The Gospel is preached here, not in Hell
9. Judgment Seat of Christ, Great White Throne Judgment
10. Saved – Judgment Seat of Christ, Lost – Great White Throne Judgment
11. whosoever, not found, book, life

12. Jesus Christ, Alpha, Omega

SECTION VII
1. Joshua
2. commanded thee, strong, good courage, afraid, dismayed, with thee
3. True
4. Unaware, weakness, doubt God's Word
5. flesh, eyes, life
6. conformed, world, transformed, renewing, mind, prove, good, acceptable
7. True, False Evidence Appearing Real
8. falling, loud noises
9. fear not, kill, not able, soul, fear, destroy, soul, body, hell
10. False
11. deny himself, take up his cross
12. Eternal Rewards, sacrificial Foundation, Soul Changing Purpose, Love Motivated Power, Timeless Endurance
13. flesh
14. walk, flesh, war, flesh, weapons, warfare, carnal, mighty, God, strong holds, imaginations, high thing, exalteth, bringing, captivity, readiness, revenge all disobedience

SECTION VIII
1. Yes
2. last, one hour, equal, borne, burden
3. True
4. c. all the above
5. your calling, wise men, flesh, mighty, noble, chosen, foolish, world, confound, weak, base, despised, not, nought, flesh, glory
6. Saul of Tarsus
7. win, satisfied

8. conformed, world, transformed, renewing, mind, prove, perfect
9. True
10. b. a. c.
11. Soul Warrior
12. Staff Evangelist
13. Saints, Overseer, Shepherd
14. time, endure sound doctrine, own lusts, heap, teachers, turn away, truth, fables, watch, endure afflictions, evangelist, full proof
15. Staff Evangelist, True

SECTION IX

1. Yes
2. True
3. thing, doest, not good, wear away, thou, this people, too heavy, able, thyself alone
4. main thing
5. b. find those who will answer the call
6. apostles, prophets, evangelists, pastors, teachers, perfecting, saints, work, edifying
7. Trespassing
8. d. all the above
9. aggressive planned out mission
10. All power, heaven, earth, Go ye, teach, nations, baptizing, Father, Son, Holy Ghost, commanded you, alway
11. People, know, way, humility, Obedience, believing
12. heavenly joy, teach, deeply, love

SECTION X

1. Knee Shall Bow
2. e. all the above
3. Nature, Demons, Death, Hell
4. True

5. wrestle, flesh, blood, principalities, powers, rulers, darkness, world, spiritual wickedness
6. 1:4, 1:5
7. non-existent, pure deception
8. doers, word, hearers, deceiving, hearer, doer, beholding, natural face, goeth, forgetteth, manner, was
9. No
10. True
11. Way, Truth, Life
12. True
13. True
14. servant, highways, hedges, compel, come in

SECTION XI

1. word, God, quick, powerful, sharper, sword, piercing, dividing asunder, soul, spirit, joints, marrow, thoughts, intents
2. True
3. "Thy word is a lamp unto my feet, and a light unto my path." "The entrance of thy words giveth light; it giveth understanding unto the simple."
4. False
5. Boring, Irrelevant
6. True
7. Jesus Return, Saved, Heaven
8. Almighty God
9. Joel, Acts 2:16-21
10. Saved, Baptized
11. Christ, new creature, passed away, new
12. True
13. Lamb's, Book, Life
14. reconciliation
15. reconcile, conform

16. workmanship, good works, ordained, walk, them
17. True
18. Courage, Promise
19. Staff Evangelist, Great Commission

SECTION XII

1. True
2. spiritual depression, apathy and gross sin, conscious of backslidden condition, yearn for God's power, leaders have a prophetic insight (any three)
3. peace, sword
4. Engaging, Plan, Faith
5. faith, works, dead, faith, works, by my
6. gates of hell shall not prevail against the church
7. combine efforts, knees, prayer, culture
8. grain, mustard seed
9. grain, mustard seed, sowed, field, least, seeds, grown, greatest, becometh, tree, lodge, branches
10. Eternal, Holy Spirit
11. fruit, righteous, tree, life, winneth souls, wise
12. Great Commission
13. Yes

www.ingramcontent.com/pod-product-compliance
Lightning Source LLC
Chambersburg PA
CBHW071307110426
42743CB00042B/1205